I0554806

OVERCOMING
ADVERSITY

Journey of an orphan who never forgot where he came from

Dr. Russell R. Blair DNP MSN-Ed RN

To my family who support me through all life's journeys.

Leanne, Anthony, Zachary, Brittany, Katie, Hadley Rose, Amelia Rose, Makenna Ashley, and Oliver Tobias.

You are the loves of my life. You keep my light shining.

You are my purpose!

To my former nursing students and current nursing students.

To those who struggle, those with dreams, those in darkness, and those who seek a place of peace so they can shine their light and fulfill their purpose.

This book is for you.

To those who adopt. Thank you!

In Memory

of

My parents **Raymond S. and Rose A. Blair** because without them only God knows where I would be.

"You are awesome Dr. Russ!!! You have educated, advocated, taught, and inspired many nurses, including myself as I conquered through LPN to RN and now BSN!!! You are the best!!!" Dr. Russ from day one inspired, educated and advocated for not only me but for all of nursing. Present nurses, future nurses and advancing nurses.

Dr. Russ always showed support and kindness."

Danielle Heller RN (former student)

"Dr. Russell Blair has been an important influence throughout my academic and professional journey in nursing. As an educator, he served as an essential mentor to his students through his profound support and encouragement. After graduation, Dr. Blair continued to be a strong advocate in my professional growth as I started my career in nursing. I can say without hesitation that I would not be the nurse I am today without both the support and guidance I have received from Dr. Blair."

Joshua Drake BSN RN (former student)

TABLE OF CONTENTS

About the Author

Dr. Blair completed an associate in science (nursing) degree at Excelsior University in 1982. He is a graduate of the University of Phoenix, completing a Bachelor of Science (nursing) degree and a Master of Science (nursing) degree with a concentration in education. Dr. Blair attended Capella University and completed a Doctor of Nursing Practice degree (with Distinction).

Dr. Blair has devoted most of his nursing career to correctional health care. During his tenure with the Department of Corrections and Community Supervision, he served as a nurse II, nurse administrator, and regional health services administrator. Dr. Blair was employed as a Correctional Facility Specialist in the forensic/medical unit for the State Commission of Corrections.

Dr. Blair earned certification as a Correctional Health Professional. He has served as a national correctional health care surveyor, lead surveyor, and correctional health care consultant. Dr. Blair is a member of Capella University Nursing Honor Society, Sigma Theta Tau International (Omega Gamma Chapter), American Association for Men in Nursing, is a Luther Christman Fellow and a member of NurseCon.com

Dr. Blair entered academia in 2015 as an adjunct clinical instructor and retired in 2020 from his position of Associate Professor and Associate Dean of Nursing. Dr. Blair serves as a nurse planner and author at NurseCon and adjunct professor for Franklin University. Student's success and nursing support remain Dr. Blair's primary focuses.

Dr. Blair is a national presenter in correctional health care and NurseCon at Sea educator. He is co-author of NCCHC's publication; Suicide Prevention Resource Guide (National Response Plan for Suicide Prevention in Corrections). His doctoral project; Confronting Polypharmacy in Corrections: An Interprofessional Team Approach is on file in the Virginia Henderson repository.

"He is like a tree planted beside flowing streams that bears its fruit in its season and whose leaf does not wither. Whatever he does prospers."

Psalms 1:3

Introduction

There is Always Light

I have written this introduction so many times since I settled into writing for you during the summer of 2018. This was prior to the death of my mother who passed away on March 12th, 2019. Her death was and continues to be an adversity I endeavor to overcome. I will share that experience with you later in this book. While developing each chapter and writing each word, it became apparent and necessary that this book provide some form of hope, a path to a brightness for your future and a promise of better days. My hope and intention is that I provide you with some tools you can use that will help you move into the light and out of your darkness. So you can achieve your dreams. This memoir has developed into what may be an inspirational and, in some ways, spiritual guide for you. I want you to feel better about yourself when you have finished reading. The journey has been therapeutic for me. By the end, I want you to "never forget where you came from."

It was late in the summer or early fall of 2016 when I heard a local artist's original song. I was mesmerized by the passion in which the artist was presenting each word. In many ways I was able to not only hear what was being sung, but to feel the pain each word reflected. My soul had been touched by the raw feelings being shared through his music. I was saddened, and in some respects able to connect with what was being shared in his words. I appreciated the painful experience being shared so openly through song and had somehow been through similar pains myself. How I wanted to make a difference and matter to someone, anyone. I recalled the times I had caused pain for myself and even for others but now I wanted to know how I could help others who struggle and feel they are stuck in darkness to find their place in the light.

The words "In the Light" were the foundation and motivation for this book. Something I had heard several years ago has kept me moving forward on completing this project. The intensity of the song inspired me to develop my writing and to hopefully make others aware that their past is important but does not have to be the only foundation of their future.

Our adversities can be blessings we often may not recognize until many years later. There are ways to overcome the darkest of times. And one important and necessary avenue is to **"Never forget where you came from."** As you move through this book, I hope you will see how important it is to live by these words. It may impact how you identify with the present and seek your future. This would be especially true for student and nursing student readers. Please remember these words when you complete your educational journey. Never forget where you came from. Be generous with sharing your knowledge with those coming behind you. Our adversities can lead us to successes and the obstacles of our past do not have to be the foundation we build future adversity on but build our successes on. We can use adversity to build hope and achieve our dreams. Don't be an adversity for others. Allow them time to grow. Be their support and not the one who destroys their dreams. Allow them their time in the light.

I know I will reflect on some amazingly wonderful memories and most assuredly go through some dark places as I move through this book. Many of which I have traveled alone and perhaps in some ways, you may have experienced similar adversities and also traveled alone. Where does a person begin when attempting to find their inner peace, love, purpose, and a way to inspire others? How do we change the insignificance? How can we become a light? I hope we can discover this together as we move forward.

Don't misunderstand, it is not that I haven't had many years of inner peace, love, or purpose, but it was during the dark times I was able to see the brightest of light. Call me a dreamer, but I believe we can find our light during some of the darkest points in life. I believe everyone has significance. It is our responsibility and obligation to develop our self-determination to keep moving forward and not let our past or present pain determine where we can ultimately go. It may have been better for me to start such a project several years ago, but I would not have had the experiences, achievements, and faithful foundation that I have today. It is my desire that what I write can help you find your light and keep you focused on discovering your purpose and achieving your dreams.

A group of former students during their final clinical experience, a few weeks prior to graduation asked, "What words of wisdom do you have for us?" Sometimes it is the people we meet along the way who inspire us to feel free to be open in sharing ourselves in a way that may help them become aware of their potential and discover what may lay undiscovered in them. My silence was extended, and perhaps beyond what they had determined as an appropriate amount of time to respond to their question, and apparently, I was correct. One student finally stated, *"I guess he doesn't have any words of wisdom for us."* I am certain he didn't realize this was not an easy question and I wanted to provide them with somewhat of an intelligent response. After all, I was their professor and we had spent weeks together.

Finally completing my exercise of deep thought, my response to those in the clinical group was very simple. *"Never forget where you came from."* Those six words had an impact on those eight students and will remain the foundation as I move forward in this book. They understood what I was saying and could finally see the wisdom in what I was sharing. Thankfully!

If through some of my life experiences, someone can learn they also can succeed and achieve their wildest dreams then I have achieved my goal and achieved the inner peace, love, and purpose I am seeking through this project. It is my expectation that through this book I can open my heart and allow others to see an existence that will bring life on the inside for them and help move them into their light. Perhaps my story will be an inspiration for others to move forward and achieve all that has been placed on the road ahead for them. I do not believe my life is any more important, special, or amusing than yours, but I have a story to tell and maybe through sharing I can inspire you to always reach for your dreams. I continue to reach for mine even today. As I told mom, who was 93 when I started this project. "I still don't know what I want to be when I grow up". Mom has been gone four years now, I am still writing this book, and I still don't know what I want to be when I grow up.

I am fortunate to be loved by a wonderful woman and mother of my two loving and amazing sons. Leanne has been and always will be the most supportive person in my life and in the lives of so many others (I know mom looks down and smiles on her each day). Even when I may not have deserved her support. Leanne gave it freely. I am sure others have felt the same during their journey. Of all the people having an impact in my life she remains at the top of the list. In all these years, she has lived to provide her inspiration so that others can be in the light. Leanne has always supported me moving forward and allowed me to enjoy the brightest of light. I really do share the light with her. She is one of the best nurses and patient advocates any patient could desire. She has always been the best wife, mother, daughter, and daughter-in-law. This book must also be a part of her light. A greater part of our lives has moved forward together, than we ever did alone.

When I began this project I did not have any intention of it being my memoir or being of a spiritual nature. While writing I felt the deepest desire to associate some scriptural and motivational references throughout. It is my book after all and I believe if you read each reference I have selected they will provide you a different perspective on your adversities as they have mine. They certainly have been an inspiration for me and at times they were exactly what I needed. My faith continues to move me forward, and in all ways keeps my feet firmly planted. Some days the ground is a bit shaky, but when I don't have or believe I have anything else, I have my faith. I continue to stumble and fall. And so will you. I have learned how to be unsuccessful at my first attempt and keep moving forward. I am certain that without my foundation of faith, I could never have achieved what I have in life. I continue to need spiritual guidance through many situations, nearly daily. I do believe it is through my faith, spiritual power and certainly God's grace that strengthens me. If I can be in the light, through "Never forgetting where I came from." So can you! As we move forward, I hope you can discover your hope and find encouragement in what I will share. That you too can finally have a life in the light while overcoming your darkness, obstacles and adversities and keep moving forward.

It doesn't matter what you are going through, you can overcome adversity. When you feel overwhelmed, remind yourself of your power through faith. As a result of this you are greater than any adversity you face. You will be an Overcomer!

"In the same way, let your light shine before others, so that they may see your good works and give glory to your father in heaven."

Matthew 5:16

I

Unwanted

I want to start telling you my story because it has something that only you might relate with. Have you ever felt unwanted? Perhaps you have, because almost everyone has had that feeling at some point. Have you ever thought what it would be like to be unwanted at birth? I suspect many will have no idea.

Here is a shadow that has been with me all my life and I know that is why I am finally putting down these words. Even though I am grateful that this shadow led me to find the greatest blessing I have ever known I should not hesitate talking about it still. Even though this shadow gave way to a purpose for the rest of my life, there was a time when it stood in my way, blocking the light of love.

And yet, I have none to blame for what I am going to say happened to me. I have only to thank God, my spiritual provider and my parents, who took it upon themselves to nurture the baby from the day they adopted him. I realize now, more than ever, that there is a reason behind every situation to occur. When the woman who bore me gave me away at birth; even that had its purpose no matter the length of years it took me to recognize it.

Poverty is the greatest of all ills, they say. Some have gone farther to say that the only major sin in life is to be poor. That means society never forgives you for being poor. I would like to take a moment to ponder how tough it might have been financially for the woman who brought me into this world.

Perhaps she was unwed at the time and circumstance did not leave her any choice but to give up her newborn. Looking inward, I am sure I have no animosity now because I can imagine it must not have been an easy decision on her part. I am actually thankful no other alternatives were resorted to. Thankfully, it was adoption I awaited and nothing else!

I close my eyes and imagine a huge medical center and no one else besides the nursing staff to care for me. And yes, it is no wonder I am settled with the profession I am in today because the very first hand that touched me to keep me warm and feed me was the hand of a nurse.

They named me Edward and so Edward was left behind by his real parents because he was unwanted. Like the way you feel when a package you receive isn't really what you wanted. You stick a return label on it and send it back.

Since my mom's death in March 2019, I have discovered my complete given name at the time of birth. At this stage in my life that fact has no meaning, bearing, or impact on where I have been or where I am headed. That period of my life has been completed and is simply the past. It cannot be changed, so I will focus on the future. I am aware not all adopted individuals may feel the same. It is my desire to just move forward. I have no idea where I lived or with whom I lived for these first few months of my life.

Edward remained unwanted until he was around six months old.

I was born in a county over an hour away from the county my adoptive parents lived. Thankfully there was a connection. What, where, when, and how; all of that will continue to be a mystery for the rest of my days. I lack any desire to have these and many more questions answered. I remain thankful that I was offered for adoption and not aborted.

So, what happens to those unwanted at birth? Is there something you feel inside forever or perhaps you never feel anything? Unwanted! Is it the start of a trend for the rest of that person's life? I think I will attempt to explain such questions later.

I have known the love of awesome parents but I am not sure I ever experienced loving myself. I had the 'return' label stuck on me but of course I couldn't be sent back to a factory to be dissembled with parts of me incorporated into something else later. Okay, so I sort of like sat in the 'damaged goods' area at the customer service counter in a store until someone walked up and said, "Hey, I think I can do something useful with it. I'll take it." Don't let hearing me say that make you think I voice pity for myself. But I do wonder if that 'return' or 'unwanted' label can travel internally with such a newborn for a lifetime? In some respects, I believe it may.

At the same time I hope you, who are reading this, have reached a point where it will stop having a lasting impact on the rest of your life. Life hung in the balance for me when I was born and I could only wait for my status to change from unwanted to that of wanted. I hung in the balance of a system which you could only hope made the right decision for someone so young and vulnerable. Our foster care system is so heartbreaking.

There are so many people who want to raise children yet it is almost always a baby they want to get. Very few accept the truth that children can be a blessing no matter what their age. Imagine the departments charged with allowing immigration into their country suddenly decided grownup immigrants cannot contribute to the economy and the social fabric so they should only be allowing immigration starting from birth? Would that make any sense?

I am a supporter of adoption and know that if people opened their hearts, we could work toward improving the foster care system today. I wish I were younger. I know I would open my heart and my home to more children.

"You saw me before I was born. Every day of my life was recorded in your book. Every moment was laid out before a single day had passed."

Psalm 139:16

5

Fortunately for me I chose to not allow the "unwanted" label to control my direction in life. And that label appeared repeatedly to stall the progress I wanted to make. I fought against the perspective that label projected: I did not make the mark from the start so any outcome following that simply cannot change. It is mainly a question of whether you allow the unwanted to control you or step up to control the unwanted instead.

Now the question may be: how could I refuse the unwanted to control my life as an infant?

Our walls of protection are how we survive from the beginning and how we learn to move forward. I know my wall of protection was provided by my God. He found someone here to take over for Him because I went from that hospital nursery into the arms of a wonderful family. What else but His Grace could have made me able to achieve what I have in life and grant me the ability to share this experience with and hopefully inspire you?

I will support many of the things I talk about throughout this book with a response from a good and powerful reference. Thankfully my belief is in a good and forgiving God. Yet, I can tell you that throughout this sharing I may have more questions than answers. I simply hope to discover the light.

I just had no idea what I really wanted from life. I knew I was one of the luckiest newborns in that nursery. Is there a connection between being unwanted at the start and not having any awareness of what you truly desire later in life? But what you desire on the inside may never be brought to life. We have all desired something during our lives – a new job, a country home, a mansion on a hill. Should I remain in a dark place if my mansion never came?

I know today had I not been motivated to complete school and keep moving forward, my desire on the inside of being a teacher would not have been completed.

Let me take you back to my teenage years for just a moment. After recording my first record (you will learn more about my singing career in a later chapter), a 45 RPM vinyl (the CD of the 1970s) in 1975, at age 15 I went to visit my grandfather in Pennsylvania. I even remember the floor plan of the house he lived in. You entered the back door into the kitchen slightly to the right. You walked straight from the back door you found the bathroom. To the left you walked through the bedroom and went

7

out to a porch living room area. Not a large home at all. But a place I have visited in recent years.

The unwanted child played the record for grandpa, and it was an immediate hit. My grandfather's wife said to him, "I told you Joe he would turn out to be something." I wasn't sure what he may have said in the past and my musical career never blossomed, but for the next few days he traveled me around Pennsylvania into every hotel and bar he could find to have me play my guitar and sing. Apparently, I had proven to be someone he could have some pride in. I hope he is still proud today. Many years later it was explained that my grandfather didn't want my mom to adopt children as that meant you were getting someone else's problem. I am glad that was just a myth and that his daughter chose not to listen.

On a subsequent trip we arrived to find grandpa had passed away an hour before we arrived in town. That vacation was spent making funeral arrangements and burying the grandfather who hadn't thought I would amount to anything. I was sad and have 'never forgotten where I came from'.

Through the years I have been asked many times; "Don't you want to know about your parents?" I can tell you without a doubt, I know everything there is to know about my parents.

I have progressed enough in life to know I am not damaged goods (my God loves all) and certainly my life has been and continues to be much better than it may have been had the circumstances at birth or before birth been different. Completely realizing that giving birth does not make you a mother I am aware my adoptive parents provided much peace, love, and purpose to my life as an infant and well into my adulthood. As I examine my life through this journey, they continue to provide my peace, love, and purpose even today.

I will call my spiritual provider, God. You should feel free to use your own provider of spiritual strength as applicable in your life and situation(s). I strongly believe we need a connection with some form of spiritual being to guide us. Mine is of a spiritual and religious nature. I encourage you to find yours. If we do share the same God, you will understand and be helped more from what I write. If you need a spiritual guide, I will suggest you try mine. He helps!

*"**Give justice to** the poor and the **orphan**; uphold the rights of the oppressed and the destitute. Rescue the poor and helpless; deliver them from the grasp of evil people."*

Psalm 83:3-4

II

Chosen

The couple who chose to have me was looking to adopt a baby girl. Their caseworker approached them about a baby boy. They may have passed it up but fortunately for me, they said yes.

The same caseworker came up to them some years later and that time they were waiting for another boy. The caseworker said to them if they would take a little girl. My sister was four and had been in the foster care system for some time. We were both lucky orphans. The couple who wanted a daughter would select a son and later the same couple wanting a boy would select a daughter.

The house dad built had only two bedrooms. It wouldn't be until we were older that dad put an addition on the house, so we didn't have to share a bedroom like Sheldon and Missy.

11

I must have arrived at my patents' place in the winter although my birthday falls in August. Mom told me how much I hated the snowsuit she had to put me in. I would give her a hard time because I've never liked winter and being bundled up. I still have that snowsuit and I am still not a proponent of the snowsuit or winter.

So, out of all the babies and children it was I whom my parents chose. 'The Chosen One'; words I would use again with the opportunities that came my way many years after my chosen status. At this point, I will reinforce my perspective of divine intervention.

*"I knew you before I formed you in your mother's womb. Before you were born, **I set you apart** and appointed you as my prophet to the nations."*

Jeremiah 1:5

Thus, the transition from 'unwanted' to 'chosen'. There are many references in the Bible for 'chosen'.

*But **you are a chosen generation,** a royal priesthood, a holy nation, His own special people, that you may proclaim the praises of*

Him who called you out of darkness into his marvelous light.

1 Peter 2:9

Perhaps you wouldn't expect to have scripture quoted in a book that started with a rundown on the persistence of dark places and beginning life unwanted – but, what better time and place to try realizing there is a bigger plan for everyone? You will see that the shield of protection God has around us gets us through many situations as you continue this journey with me.

Blessed is the nation whose God is the Lord, ***the people He has chosen as His own inheritance.***

Psalms 33:12

How lucky can you get?

Life was going to be some adventure – not for me yet, as I was only starting out, but definitely for my parents.

Was my mother not able to bear a child? Mom was always an anxious woman. A strong woman in all respects, but nervous. I'm not sure where the anxiety came from, but it had managed to stick with her throughout her life. She chose to adopt over giving birth because she had experienced her own adversities with a sisters' difficult pregnancy and the loss of an aunt at age twenty-one following childbirth. Mom and dad were in their early thirties when they made the decision to adopt. Mom was certainly a bible believing and faith-filled woman, but anxiety was a major part of her life from her mid-forties on.

My mom could have had her own baby, as far as the very squeamishly unadventurous definition of 'my own baby' should go. In her case, her own baby was me.

"Anxiety is not only a pain which we must ask God to assuage, but also a weakness we must ask Him to pardon."

C.S. Lewis

She had her fearful moments learning to care for a newborn child. She told me stories of how she managed to stab me with a diaper pin (there were no disposable diapers back then), then nearly drowning me when she hadn't put the nipple on a bottle correctly. I was discovered gurgling as the formula poured all over my face.

Despite all such occurrences, life was good. I had a warm home, and I was kept clean and fed. God no doubt blessed me with my parents and I truly was the chosen one.

"Don't worry about anything; instead, pray about everything. Tell God what you need and thank him for all he has done."

Philippians 4:6

"Give your entire attention to what God is doing right now, and don't get worked up about what may or may not happen tomorrow. God will help you deal with whatever hard things come up when the time comes."

Matthew 6:34 (MSG)

My sister and I can clearly recall that the home we were placed in is where all our dreams came true and there was never a time we were wanting for anything.

"Look at the birds of the air, for they neither sow nor reap nor gather into barns; yet your heavenly Father feeds them. Are you not of more value than they?"

Matthew 6:26 (NKJV)

Of course, all the tribulations you can expect going through childhood came our way but the happy times will never stop outweighing any bad patches that may have fallen along the way. In our memories, our home was warm and welcoming. We were fortunate our mom was a housewife and a mother. Between her and dad, her job was much harder. Dad worked full time in a paper-mill. He was the provider and he took care of his family without exception.

We attended church every Sunday as a family. Sunday school was part of the routine followed by a nice dinner always prepared by mom, cleaned up by dad and then there was dad's weekly Sunday ride. At the time our parents were both smokers. Medical science did not have a big impact on smoking at the time. So, we enjoyed hours in the car with the smoke billowing out of the partially open car windows.

Following the ride, family night on Sunday gave way to the Wonderful World of Disney and sometimes Lawrence Welk. We watched television as a family and the evening would bring dad's western eggs or popcorn.

This eventually became special pizza night. First, out of a Chef Boyardee box and later my sister and I made the pizza after we learned how to while working during our teen years in a local restaurant.

We enjoyed family vacations and camping during the summers. Reels of film have preserved our childhood memories with family and friends. Those were days when you enjoyed birthdays with family and made memories at home.

When either of us stepped out line, we were disciplined. But the worst part was when we had to go pick our own disciplinary device out of the lilac bush. Not that there were sessions of heavy beatings at the hands of either dad or mom, but they knew how to make us behave appropriately in public. It did keep us out of trouble most of the time.

Today, my sister and I would want our mom and dad to be just the way they were if we could go back and do it all over. I would even cherish one of those Sunday rides with our parents funking the car with their cigarette smoke. At times I believe our lives surpassed those of families whose children were born directly into the family.

Dad's parents had passed before my adoption, and I have no recollection of them. Mom's parents and grandparents were alive when we arrived in the family. There was never a doubt we were the grandchildren and great-grandchildren of mom's side of the family (at least her mom, stepfather, and grandparents). Our adoptions were never a secret, and we were accepted as received. One of dad's brothers did come to the house when I arrived home. He wanted to meet his new nephew. Dad always spoke about this visit. I think he was proud. Never for a moment did the unwanted label return. We were chosen and became a family.

I wish I could tell all of the wonderful stories from those days in the pages of this book. But I must talk about this one on one of my birthdays when we returned to my grandparents' house from camping. As soon as we pulled into the driveway, the automatic garage door rose and there stood a glistening red Honda 50 cc minibike – three speed with all the bells and whistles. Happy Birthday!

I could not wait to pry myself from the birthday hugs and ride it. When I finally revved it and made rounds around the yard, my sister stared wide-eyes at the scene. I stopped in front of her and she hopped on smiling but my parents could see her disappointment. Within hours we were at the dealership and my sister got a shiny yellow one to match mine.

Living in the country we had plenty of land to ride on. We were kids, and sometimes the road provided a much softer riding experience. Shh! don't tell.

As we grew to school age, our Sunday evenings following Wonderful World of Disney would be bath night. I must repeat, bath, in a tub. No shower. Then pulling on our PJs, into bed for a good night's sleep before waking up early the next morning for school. We'd get dressed and wait at the end of the driveway for the school bus.

The more I try to remember what I had for breakfast during my school years, the more I believe I did not eat any. It must not have sat well in a stomach upset by default in the morning, causing me to forego it entirely lest the rest of the school day was spent in torment.

I hated peanut butter and jelly for lunch and usually we had a cheese sandwich with butter and mustard, and a bag of chips. I will sometimes still make a cheese sandwich. Never forget where you came from.

There was one occasion when the school district tried to change the school bus pick-up location from the end of our driveways to the end of our road. The parents in the

19

neighborhood staunchly refused to allow any of the kids to stand in the dark at the end of a country road. Even so, those days a dark county road was safe. The school district never tried doing it again. We were picked up for school at the end of our driveways until each of us became old enough to drive to school.

So I made it from being left alone to being with a family for whom a small thing like where I waited for the school bus to arrive mattered.

Living through our frailties makes evident how powerfully spiritual belief can be shaped within our heart. The ability of God to carry us through the bleakest hour demonstrates His power. By relying on Him we are the chosen generation, called out of darkness and into marvelous light.

We must never relinquish hope even if we have to fight for it to the very last. Caring for others more than we do for ourselves is the essence of love.

III

Underachiever

School never failed to fuel the emptiness inside me. I don't think it would have been evident on the outside. The emptiness was something I could touch, like one might touch solid, shiny, reinforced glass. That glass was set up to guard the emotions which lay behind it – never letting anyone through in case the emotions found an escape route. Those were days I simply lived with it.

Back in the small town nestled away in its peaceful county, the bus rode me to the four-room schoolhouse where I attended kindergarten. I guess they call it the foundation year or some revamped term to give it a facelift for latter-day urban gentry.

I wasn't someone who looked forward to taking that bus ride. Yet, I remember Mrs. Hunt who had the uncanny talent to make school feel like home. If it wasn't for her

21

heartfelt influence at such an incipient period of my life, I would not have poured my heart into teaching later in life.

I will never forget her because she is part of the pieces making up where I came from.

I still keep a wooden box and I open it sometimes like I'm doing now. Its contents consist of the hiccupping school career that stalked me from kindergarten all the way to high school. Looking at the pile of report cards, I can now take the time to appreciate how I was observed by my academic superiors. It can be funny looking at the remarks immortalized in dried ink. Sometimes it can conjure up some of the darkest times in my life.

Here's number seven: I respond to music. My eyes trace over the 'very well' and the 'B' or 'better than satisfactory' for almost all the school subjects.

Here's number six: I can skip. Not yet improving; still trying – I am sure Mrs. Hunt would have been proud by the time I got to senior year and learned how to skip quite fine. Even though my fine was something she would hardly have endorsed.

I played hooky from my homeroom class whenever I thought I should. Many a day I would arrive late to school and on days when the weather was nice, I dropped the idea altogether. I'm not sure mom knew about it.

Thinking back, what wouldn't I give to have my rug and lay on the floor of that kindergarten classroom once more? Once my days with Mrs. Hunt in that tiny cabinet of a schoolhouse were over, school life was never the same.

First grade was a dismal time. My motivation was always on the run from me and the final note from the teacher says I needed to be 'pushed constantly'. I suspect I was lucky to finally see the second grade classroom at all. Sitting still was a monumental task and I could never wrap my head around the idea of taking school seriously.

If you pushed my school years down to the present time, they wouldn't waste time pronouncing me as having ADHD (Attention Deficit Hyperactivity Disorder). The notes on my report cards hold up to it.

Third grade brought disaster and the first major failure of my life. It was the first major adversity where I had more U's than I did S's; and I was absent thirty-two half-days from school. I had to give that grade a second chance.

Why was I out of school so much? It will remain a mystery. Yet, I know that even though I was unsuccessful, I wasn't a failure, because I improved enough to be promoted the second time around.

Fourth grade saw my attendance growing but I became a slacker as the year progressed. Here's my social studies score in November: A- and by June I'm able to squeak by with a D. Anyway, they hauled me along to the fifth grade.

I wonder if the school administration did it out of kindness or pity. Maybe someone who counted thought I should be promoted on the basis of ability. They could not have been mentally hampered enough to do it because they detected any motivation. My motivation avoided me like the plague.

Yet, fifth grade brought a teacher whose class I enjoyed. What's more? He was able to get me to do my work. Then sixth grade came and went; not always seeing me doing my best – the teachers almost scavenging for my attention in the classroom.

By the end of the year I must have been attentive enough to warrant my promotion to junior high school. I'm thinking again about the *labels* that observations reported in these report cards would provide me with today.

School athletics and PE (physical education) made me feel frozen. It just was not for me. Of course, if you weren't a *jock* you had to be a *fag*. Gay wasn't a descriptive term much used in the '70s. Queer was the word of choice and it hurt.

I recall one PE class where we were on the archery range. I shot an arrow into the sky. It came down and struck the high school building shy of the door.

At some point in my early teens I was lucky to sustain a knee injury during summer camp. God does work in mysterious ways. It was my ticket out of PE for the rest of high school. The adversity of a severe injury made me successfully avoid PE! You see it is all in your perspective. It only became a problem when it kept bothering me into adulthood. It raised its ugly head again when I took up downhill snow skiing. Can you imagine that? A guy who hates winter chooses downhill skiing? As I was not built for exertion of that kind it did not

25

become my sport of choice either. Nonetheless it was fun while it lasted.

I did enjoy attending high school basketball games, football games, homecoming, and other school events. But they were not fun attending if you went alone. I also enjoyed watching and supporting the New York Yankees. Yes, I still support the Yankees today. I just didn't want to play.

I was an underachiever par excellence, if you please. Even something as simple as 'skipping' could not get my motivation going. My elementary school years did see me having an interest in music; it was noticed as early as kindergarten. This interest would not develop further until junior high. That is when I tried taking an interest in the school choir, but the choir director was not interested in me.

Social life was bland if it existed at all during my school years. I didn't belong anywhere, and I knew it. Later in my high school years I did join a local drum corps and served as an assistant drum major. That experience filled the empty times and gave me a group of friends and extended family. Some that I still have today.

But if I try to talk about something special related to my classmates or what we kids would do after school, I have nothing. I had no friends who formed a constant part of my life back then. There was no one in my class whom I would think of as my companion. The adversity was my sole companion. Existing on the fringe was my only identity moving into teenage years.

Yes, there were family friends I went camping with during summer, but besides that temporary outing I was alone for much of the year. School and home were totally different environments. School gave me upset stomachs most of the time and home was always my safe place.

I was the medium-stature *husky* kid. My goodness, I can even remember my aunt making a pair of pants with an elastic waistband for me. They were light tannish orange corduroy (can you imagine?). She was a great seamstress, and it was a nice gesture. Not sure if mom picked them up as a nice gesture or if it was because I was the so-called husky boy. My aunt sewed a variety of items as I recall, and some were very nice. But I hated those pants and everything they stood for. This husky boy couldn't wear a pair of store-bought trousers. This fat boy just didn't like going to the gym. Not to mention I didn't want to parade around naked in front of

27

anyone. I hated gang showers; they just didn't seem natural or right to me. Case closed.

When I think back on junior high school, I only remark by saying: wow! No more grade school and ready to conquer the world, we were the big kids on campus attending classes on the bottom level of the high school building. We didn't realize at the time that in spite of our inflated sense of confidence, the laugh was on us. The bottom level was pretty much our area because we didn't mingle often with the senior high students. Lunch, PE, art and music were the only things that had us stepping out of 'our area'.

Even though I managed to pull off some good grades, I was not honor roll material. Having avoided major academic problems while moving up seventh and eighth grades helped me remain in the Regents group, but the work was demanding. Regents, is a special diploma given only in the State of New York for passing a series of standardized tests throughout high school. At the time the Regents diploma was not mandatory, and you could graduate with a school diploma.

I remained in Regents classes and was promoted to senior high with averages in the mid to upper seventies. Not bad for an unmotivated student like me.

With senior high came Math 9 (algebra). I have never been a math enthusiast, and this proved to be the year I would seal the deal. I ended the year with a 65 and scored a high of 42 on my Math 9 Regents exam. Algebra just wasn't something I could grasp. Thankfully I did later.

Since you were required to have a math for graduation, I managed a business math in tenth grade and passed with a 75. Algebra reared its ugly head again and haunted me once more in undergrad school. Yes you read that correctly. Constantly having an academic record at best fickle, I moved on to undergrad status later in life. No one could have imagined there would ever be an undergrad school for me.

A tutor helped me tackle the challenge of this phase and I ended the experience with an A in Math I, a B+ in Math II. I even finished statistics with an A, but no high school Regents diploma. I don't think it mattered. By the time eleventh grade had rolled around I was no longer interested in a Regents diploma.

What mattered was I quickly overcame that adversity. Through much of my high school journey I was reminded time and again that I was not college material. Does it sound familiar to you? I understand what it's like if it does. Don't allow those adversities to determine your future or your dreams. I think these adversities made me a better professor further down the road. That's right; a professor.

"There is nothing you will ever face that you and God can't handle. The Lord promises us He will give us the grace to bear whatever burden comes our way."

Zig Ziglar

Before moving into my junior year of high school, I had managed to convince my guidance counselor that I would like to take my junior and senior years together. I knew other students who had attempted the same academic progression and graduated early. After all, school was not a positive experience for me. Why prolong the suffering? He made it very clear on several occasions I was not college material and should seek other options for employment following graduation.

For those of you who have been in this situation would know there was no reason for me to drag out for another year. So, I did take my final two years of high school together.

It was during that year I would attend a practical nursing program at a local vocational school. At the time, you could take high school courses in the morning and attend a vocational program in the afternoon. I completed the year with an 81 average. I think that may have been the best grade in all my high school years. I chose to do it because the program would bring me the 2.5 credits I needed to graduate. When I graduated in June I had no intentions of returning for the second year of the nursing program – completing the first nursing year and surviving the disparaging comments was a miracle. How was all this going to impact me later in life?

You should always strive to do your best. When the past shows you did not reach those goals, it does not determine the possibilities of your future.

"There is a time for everything, and a season for every activity under the heavens."

Ecclesiastes 3:1 (NIV)

My father was a plant supervisor for a local paper mill, and this was where I was headed, not to college. I had my high school diploma and I was out of school. That is all I wanted to accomplish so my goal had been reached.

31

To the family's surprise, dad would have a minor heart attack and while hospitalized he received notice the paper mill was closing. He and mom were financially secure, so an early retirement was not an adversity for them. Mom knew how to manage a budget and could make the funds go a long way. A trait I know she inherited from her mother. Dad never regretted taking his retirement early. He enjoyed many wonderful years following this adversity. He was still young enough to enjoy all of the things he and mom loved doing together. It wasn't bad having both of them home.

What was I going to do now that I had completed high school? My first year of practical nursing finally saw me getting acquainted with the girl who had been chasing me all through high school.

One of her friends was the matchmaker. I was in a nursing program with not only her, but her mother. We developed a close friendship and with time began dating as well. She, her mother and a mutual friend convinced me to go back to the second year of nursing as a postgraduate student.

Since I would have originally graduated the next year from high school, the school district picked up the tab for my second year of practical nursing school. It was another intervention by God, who knows the plan.

I am certain if the school district hadn't paid the tuition, mom and dad would have generated the necessary funds. I was still living at home and working part time. As long as you were in school, you didn't have to chip in on the family budget. It seemed fair at the time. Today children might be appalled at such a structure but back then it was a very reasonable arrangement.

Out of high school early; still going to school and mom would remind me of this time to time. At my Doctoral Commencement Ceremony, she wanted to know if I was done with school yet. "You wanted out of school early and you have been going ever since," she said. How right she was.

The 1970s were difficult times. I was a male going to a nursing program and I was still not sure what the future was going to bring. Those were times when you either drowned yourself in a drug haze because you wanted to prove you didn't care where the world was headed or you proclaimed ideology to show there was nothing you couldn't understand about the future. Tending to the wounded, the frail and defenseless hardly counted as the means to make one's mark in society. Not to say such an action would not be appreciated from a moral standpoint. But could you be a successful man training as a nurse?

I have talked about my lack of motivation during middle school and high school years. My decelerated efforts toward acquiring acceptable traits as far as school activities and academics went kept me from being part of any specific social group, whether inside or outside of school. On the other hand my interest in music never became a vehicle to want to become part of a subculture, so there too I did not find a way to overstep the fence around my heart. This made me a target of negative and derogatory comments. Fag, faggot, queer, were the major descriptive terms at the time when you weren't part of the group. The remarks were not exclusively directed toward me, but at anyone who didn't move among the approved social group or was not part of an athletic program. Certainly, I didn't make the cut. Those words flowed quite easily from the mouths of classmates. The '70s slowly drew to a close but the adversities of a vulnerable population would only worsen.

I have acquaintances, colleagues, and friends from every color of the rainbow. Honestly, I think a rainbow is beautiful. Wouldn't the world be a boring place in just pink and blue? If we are created in the image of God, then a rainbow is indeed a beautiful thing. I have never seen a rainbow that wasn't beautiful. Have you? I am thankful I believe in a loving and caring God and that we all were created in his image, and he loves what he has created. We are all part of a colorful world.

I have a special place in my heart for men who enter nursing. My advice to them is to keep moving forward and make your mark in this noble profession. If only we could find it in ourselves to be kind and embrace the beauty that surrounds us. There is no need to taint that beauty with the ugliness of stereotypes.

Bullying is not something new, it has been around for decades. I have been there, and I have experienced every aspect. The words burned just as much then, as they do today. Whether it was fact or fiction didn't matter. It was not important to those who verbalized such remarks if what they were saying was true or not.

In those days it was something you could get away from. I simply went home. Not having cell phones or social media, going home resulted in a reprieve from the taunting. Sure, the words cut like a knife and burned like a hot poker. But it was not as common back then to shout for an advocate. You took the hurting in silence.

Today the words are equally hurtful but thankfully society has gained a better understanding. We continue to work toward the acceptance of the LGBTQ+ community. Probably here is where the theology scholars will close the book.

Today we need to live in a welcoming society for the benefit of everyone, more than we ever did. I have read the backs of T-shirts saying F*K your feelings. Perhaps this is what is wrong with our world today. We stop caring about one another's feelings and this is an area where individuals need advocacy to overcome the adversities they face.

It is sad that some of our youth feel they must resort to suicide when the taunting doesn't end. We hear about these incidents time and time again. When will we open our heart?

Bullying has led to 4,000 deaths annually according to the CDC. It is the third leading cause of death among young people. For every completed suicide there are 100 attempts. There were 42% of LGBTQ+ youth suicides in 2021. Why? It has gotten out of control and technology does not allow an escape for individuals who are experiencing these adversities.

If you bully someone, give it some thought. Would you want to be in the victim's shoes? And, yes they are victims of your verbal abuse. Love is love and who are any of us to judge? My friends, the LGBTQ+ community will not bully you. Just live your life. Why can't we accept one another, and move forward? Accept one another, just as Christ accepted you. It can only make the world a better place.

Accept one another, then, just as Christ accepted you, in order to bring praise to God.

Romans 15:7

In my youth I tried the Boy Scouts and that just didn't work out. It would become a very special part of my life many years later. When I joined, dad's nephew was the Scoutmaster, and his sons were in the troop. I didn't make the cut there either. I felt like an outcast at every meeting, and it was made clear that I wasn't as smart or good as anyone else in the troop. I believe today I may be the only one there who achieved a doctorate level education. Recently, one of the members of that troop stated, "Well, I won't call you doctor."

Funny thing, it doesn't matter. Sadly, this was verbalized at the most inappropriate time and allegedly by an intelligent individual. It remains a fact whether acknowledged or not. I completed a doctorate degree, and this person didn't. Perhaps that is an adversity for them to overcome.

What I didn't realize was how important my past would become in my future. Once again, I have never forgotten where I came from, and I believe that has made a difference for me today. Times such as those can only make us stronger, and they did. Never forget where you came from.

IV

Acceptance

I recall playing the usual childhood games while growing up – games like school teacher, bus driver, singer, preacher and of course the popular doctor. I didn't get much to be proud of when it came to my personal abilities but putting on shows for our parents, my sister helping me while sometimes family friends helped too, was something I always looked forward to.

It was a time I had yet to learn that failure was being unsuccessful the first time. So, all I saw was that I wasn't great at anything. Anything I accomplished would not last but I hadn't discovered myself, had I? Something did put me in the limelight, even if for a brief stint of time, during my high school era. It was the guitar. The memories swirl before my eyes as I take a look at the yearbook entries here on the table. The night outside the window is

39

quiet, but images conjured by the words signed by old school colleagues are filled with the buzz and thrum and flair of music.

You didn't need a decree from the state prosecutor's office to convince me I didn't have a properly functioning brain. I had already passed the verdict in that regard. I could not make it in athletics and lacked the desire to do so; I was husky; I didn't have any close school friends; every derogatory name you can think of had been used to accost me. When all else fails, pick up a guitar, sing a song, do a nice job and you are loved almost instantly. Sounds absurd; don't laugh, but it happened.

I really don't recall when I began to have an interest in the guitar. Perhaps it was not as dramatic as you may think, but that is how it seemed to a fifteen-year-old boy who spent most of his time alone. A close family friend and I began to play guitar and sing at about the same time. It seemed his goal was heading to Nashville.

I'm not sure, but somehow his dad believed we were in some sort of a competition with each other. It was the farthest thing from our young minds. At least, it was from mine. We both enjoyed playing and singing and we did sound good. He went on to make music a major part of his life, turning it into a part time career, doing rather well. My music was never at the same level but I accepted offers to sing at weddings. My family friend and I became part of a traveling variety show for some time, performing at orphanages, nursing homes and just about any place interested in seeing young talent from the area.

My favorite was singing for the children at St. Colman's Home. I loved to witness the joy our small show put in their lives. It's not uncommon for someone to ask me to sing at a funeral or a memorial service today. I also enjoy the chance to make an appearance in church now and then.

My parents never held back from buying toys for us. The popular toys and gadgets were available in the home for me and my sister. As I look back today, I realize I may have been taken advantage of for what I had or could have offered someone else. The toys brought in friends, but I use the word *friends* loosely. Were they real friends? My guitar became my closest friend for the greatest part of my youth.

"There are friends who destroy each other, but a real friend sticks closer than a brother."

Proverbs 18:14 (NLT)

41

People began noticing me exhibit the twin skill of singing and playing. Would I be overstating it if I said they were rapt seeing me do it? They said they liked the sound of my guitar and soon I was asked to perform a duet and a do a solo during one high school play. This play was named Godspell and I was charged with doing the song On the Willows, which was part of the story's spectacle. I immensely enjoyed performing it for the play. It was a beautiful experience, as was the song.

My days in the traveling variety show had me meet my first love; Ritzy was her name. I was dazzled and I think she liked me as well. She could dance like a princess. Hell, she looked like a princess too. We would get together socially, though nothing really came of our friendship. All of the few kids in the traveling show were around the same age. We traveled together several years and life moved on. I wonder what became of Ritzy.

There were other loves during my high school era. At least I thought at the time that I was in love with those girls. But loneliness was always around the corner. I met a friend of my sister, and she was two years older than I was; an older woman, so to speak. I don't know why I gave her my identification bracelet. I had received it from my parents as a Christmas gift. Whatever possessed me to give up a Christmas gift, especially one from my parents?

I was in love, but she wasn't. She kept my bracelet and gave me the hardest time giving it back. To this day I don't know why on earth she would want to keep it. But again, nothing ever developed between us. Funny thing is, today I am very good friends with her oldest brother. He has been like a big brother to me too. I have had the chance of seeing her in social gatherings and we have talked about the *'what ifs'* too. But it was only to elicit a few laughs and then we moved on. Never forget where you came from, you know?

Up on the stage singing the songs I loved and playing tunes that cheered the crowd, I had all eyes looking my way. But I remained alone. Being better known than I'd ever been brought forth the opportunity to enter the fold of a high school social group. Most of the cast during a stage show would go outside behind the school building in between rehearsals to light up the smorgasbord of smoking devices and let it make the rounds.

On one of these clandestine smoke-out events one of John Denver's songs would have greater meaning for me. Passing the pipe around was a ritual I took part in until graduation with the social group I had discovered. Finally, there was some type of acceptance. It didn't matter what group it was because hanging with them was better than being alone. This may not have been the best choice, but at the time it was better than having nothing. We did have some great times. More of the "not the best choices" came later in life. But I decided to enjoy where I was while I was at it. Throughout all this, that girl from high school was always by my side.

During my junior year of high school, I would seek the companionship of another girl who was a friend of my sister. Perhaps I should have stayed away from my sister's friends. This girl did agree to go to my junior prom. She was beautiful and we attended the prom, and I sang a song for the class accompanied by my guitar. It was a big hit. This is the only prom that I cannot look back on in pictures. When the camera film was taken for development, it flubbed. The same way the relationship with this girl failed to go further. But we found ourselves in the middle of nowhere on our way back from an after-prom party. Everyone had been drunk as skunks while billowing plumes of marijuana shrouded every face. It was nothing new for me even though alcohol would not arrive for me until a year or so later. We both felt a bit uncomfortable being there. Remember this was the class I had included myself in without being familiar with many of the students there? I could not drive after 9:00 p.m. at that time and cell phones were in large bags requiring to be plugged into a car's cigarette lighter (the 1970s and earlier automobiles had cigarette lighters in them. Now the same feature is called a 12-volt plug). We began our hike back to my house down a dark dirt road. There was plenty of time for the relationship to make an unexpected twist on that walk but we reached my place and I drove her home. No stone turned, if there is such a way of saying it; but it aptly frames the situation.

Life went on and we lost touch with each other. We did not attend the same school, so any relationship would have been difficult, I suspect. We did manage to run into each other later in life, both of us happening to practice as LPNs in the same local community hospital. Throughout all this, that girl from high school always wanted to be by my side.

After my big song at the prom, I had a thought. I am a dreamer. I wanted to bring in a few of my musical friends together to present a concert for the senior class. Dedicating an entire concert to the graduating class? Boy, this would be a hit! I was in junior year and graduating with the class one year ahead of me. This was too good an opportunity to miss as I could make new friends following this plan. So, I secured the help of my English teacher, who was also a music aficionado. At the time I needed a faculty advisor to move the event forward. Together we designed a simple set on stage. A classmate from my own class continued to play the matchmaker and it led to me meeting this girl whom I really began hanging out with. I had always seen us as good friends. She would come to the school in the evenings to help paint small saplings. All the saplings were made white which made the stage set reflect the colored lights we used during the show. I didn't realize it then, but do so now, that it was done out of a love deep inside her heart.

The show went on without a hitch, with me standing up there for all eyes to see. It was an amazing concert. At least, that's what I think. Okay, there was one hitch during the show: the high school principal had a meltdown because my friend had not gone to his school and was playing a concert at my high school. An illegal absence! Was the world going to end? I hope he has gotten over it.

It was an honor for me to make the arrangements for my adoptive graduating class. I sang a song to my mom and the spotlight was trained upon her during the entire song. She cried. I sang my heart out and the students loved it so much they began calling me John Denver around school. The name would stick with me through yearbook signings up until graduation time.

They liked the concert so much I was asked to present the same concert for the students in middle school. Following that whenever I walked through the middle school premises one girl would reach out and grab my shirt and nearly pull it off me. I think she loved my music and was in love with me. I felt like a "rock star." Later she would become one of my sisters-in-law. We still talk and laugh about it today. She is a wonderful and caring person.

Most of the music I played at the time was John Denver songs. His work became a part of my life. I played songs from a few other artists too, but John's songs were my favorite, and I must say I sang them well. They seemed to hold the most meaning for me, so it was easy to put my heart into the performance.

Back to this girl from high school: she and her brothers were members of a local drum and bugle corps and they would later encourage me to join. I didn't play a brass instrument and certainly couldn't play drums. Not sure how a guitar player and vocalist got involved with the organization, but I was assigned assistant drum major under the direction of a classmate who later became a friend. It was now the best of times. I was finally accepted by a group, and it was a large group. I had friends who were jocks, pot heads, nerds, brains, and some of the most popular kids around school. Still, the sense of being lonely tugged at my heartstrings. Today I realize so much of it was just inside my own head because I was a dreamer. I discovered during this same period that if you had a car you climbed up the rungs of *friends*. It was a rapid upward move. No surprise to me today; I can't recall many high school friends who were close. I suspect I just didn't care if I was being used or not at this point. Having friends for any reason seemed to be better than having none. It never occurred to me at the time but the loneliness never goes away even if you're in a house full of friends. When the people are gone the place is still empty. Today I have high school acquaintances, but none I would call close lifetime friends.

I did have wonderful family friends who remain friends today. I consider them family. I would be remiss if I did not mention some of my lifetime friends who are closer than blood ties.

Sue, Mike, Greg (God bless him. Gone too soon) and Randy. And now I have Phil (Sue's husband) who I consider family. Our families were one interwoven family and we have remained friends for a lifetime. These were not school friends, classmates, or people I would see every day. These were special friends, and you don't have many in a lifetime. We all grew up together and ultimately have grown older together. We have shared happy times camping, New Year-eve-parties and sad times through the deaths of family members. We have been together for over sixty years and our parents were together for lifetime too.

A friend loves at all times, and a brother is born from a time of adversity.

Proverbs 17:17

I am surprised how many individuals have no concept of real "lifetime friends." In this respect I did not have any adversity to overcome. These individuals remain in my life and heart today and have helped me overcome some of my adversities. Mike lives in Kentucky

49

now with his wife Sheila (a former high school classmate), but when my mom passed he walked in through the door. He knew I would need him. Sue and Phil were on the phone or with me through the entire journey of my mom's passing. They are my everlasting family; no adversities and genuine love. God's blessing to me and now my family. We have many wonderful and funny memories together and continue to make them still.

*"Friends come and friends go, but **a true friend sticks by you like family**."*

Proverbs 18:24 (MSG)

Even though I did not have any high school friends to turn to, I had one true girlfriend who always remained around.

Friendship between me and this high school girl continued to grow. She was way more interested in striking up a deal than I was; my history wasn't very good in that respect, so I wasn't quick to agree right away. Finally I accepted the *dating* title and agreed to attend her junior prom. She was a vision I didn't acknowledge or even respect at the time but she was in fact wonderful-looking. Perhaps my attending her prom made her the happiest girl in school as things between us slowly ripened.

***Show proper respect to everyone**, love the family of believers, fear God, honor the emperor.*

1 Peter 2:17

I realized she was someone who'd stick by me through thick and thin yet breaking through my own walls wasn't easy. I was immersed in my own past without any clue of what the future held. Attending my own "pity party," I remembered where I had come from and it wasn't always pleasant. Eleven years of school alone, perhaps the ending will be different? Always turned away in the past when attempting at a relationship and here stands this girl before me: a classmate, someone who idolizes me, and I don't seem to care. I was a husky kid. This girl was different; someone I could call my true friend.

She loved me when I didn't love myself and I know she still does today. We were husky together and she did everything in her power to make me happy and to love her. The day we married she was the most beautiful woman in the world. I tease her today that she has never been able to do her hair like that again. She never gives up trying.

*Then she said to him, "**How can you say, 'I love you,**' when you won't confide in me?*

51

Judges 16:15

Graduation day was arriving. I would be free! I spent the preceding days getting every signature I could in my yearbook. If you had any status in school, you could be sure "John" was coming to get your signature.

By graduation I had an identity. I was Russ, who had become "John" or "John Denver" of our high school. I know it was done in a positive and respectful way, but who was I? Everyone referred to me as Russ and several students wrote "John" or "John Denver." Although I respected his music, I wasn't him. I had gotten to this part of life wishing I was someone whom I was not.

One yearbook entry reads:

Russ, you're a fantastic musician and I am sure you'll succeed in life. You have put on some great concerts. Sometimes I really think you are John Denver. Take it easy, good luck. Dennis.

I believe I was successful in life and I appreciate Dennis's belief in me.

Another says:

Russ, "John". I'm really proud to be able to say I know John Denver II. Someday when you're rich and famous give me a yell. Take care, good luck and God bless. Love Cheryl.

Lisa wrote:

Russ, I'm glad there was our prom because that's when I got to know you. You're really fun to be with and I hope you always stay that way. Be a good boy.

So many of my classmates wrote things that really lifted me up, but it does not change the fact I was graduating high school, exiting the first phase of my life, and had no idea who I was or where I was going.

I was asked to sing at graduation and played John Denver's Friends and Back Home Again during the ceremony. It was wonderful and once again I was in the light. I was entering adulthood at eighteen years of age and completely without direction. My academic history was not a glowing one and I was unmotivated. That is what I had been told repeatedly and now I had to completely agree. Things would change and I would: **"Never Forget Where I Came From."** Being in the light if only for a few moments was so very wonderful. My mom and dad were always proud of my sister and I, even with the smallest of accomplishments.

Perhaps because of God's grace in lifting me above the darkness and showing me mercy, I am able to extend that mercy to others. I offer this **kindness** and **compassion** to anyone who is battling darkness. It has made my academic service rewarding.

*"God opposes the proud but **shows favor to the humble**."*

James 4:6

The Dreamer

"You say I'm a dreamer, but I'm not the only one. I hope someday you'll join us. And the world will live as one."

John Lennon

As a young man I saw visions. It's decidedly distinct from hallucinating. As an older man I dreamed. Well, not in a spiritual way, but regarding how I have attempted to live. Dreams are the essence behind our waking life, I believe. Without being able to harbor dreams we can never set sight on the things we want to achieve. Each one of us is meant for greatness, but few of us dare to live what we have dreamt. Our dreams provide us purpose. Focus too much on what has been, and we crudely let indifference eat into a vision for what is going to be.

It is essential to move from our darkness and awaken from our nightmares so we can establish the foundation for our visions and continue to build our future and live to see our dreams. You can achieve your dreams if you are willing to pay the price. Draw from the strength you are promised. Nothing is impossible.

As you establish each vision for yourself, it will become the light helping you move ahead into whatever future you choose. Your happiness is about you and only adversity can teach you the art of happiness. From being unwanted to the chosen one; from underachiever to finding acceptance – in all of this it is necessary to be a dreamer and so I was it.

*"And afterward, I will pour out my Spirit on all people. Your sons and daughters will prophesy, your **old men will dream dreams, your young men will see visions**.*

Joel 2:28

*"In the last days, God says, I will pour out my Spirit on all people. Your sons and daughters will prophesy, **your young men will see visions, your old men will dream dreams**.*

Acts 2:17

56

Following high school graduation life moved on and I kept up. I attended the second year of practical nursing, soon securing a part-time private duty case as a home health aide. My training during that time qualified me to sit with an elderly gentleman in a nearby community. He seemed a nice man from what I can recall, me being his companion mostly in the evenings. But I quickly realized home health aide and private duty were not for me. The doubt whether nursing was for me plagued me too. A teenage boy in nursing school in the '70s: you know what stemmed from that as I have already shared the experience with you.

Today, as I suspected even then, people understand men have been in nursing for hundreds of years so I wasn't the first. Some of my nursing students would tell you Florence Nightingale and I attended nursing school together. So why did it seem like such a new thing back then? Why were males who entered nursing tormented and ridiculed? Overcoming adversities is the name of this book. It was just another adversity I had to overcome, and I didn't stop moving. And once again I ask, why?

Graduation from nursing school was just around the corner and I wanted a job in a community hospital. Long-term care was not my passion. We had experienced that throughout most of the nursing program. I had my eye on a new car. I looked at a new Buick Skylark, right on the showroom floor. It was beautiful, red with a white interior and white landau roof and with my parents' help, I bought the car. Now I really needed that job. I determined the job was of greatest importance now, and later it would be a major part of my calling. I headed off to a larger community and knocked on the door of the local community hospital. I completed the application process and was hired as an LPN in the pediatric unit. I secured the job explaining to the interviewer I would want to return for my RN. LPNs at that time were a valued commodity in the community hospital setting. The job was necessary and all about returning to school. I was primarily interested in paying for the new car. Believe me at that time I had no desire to return to school. I did need the position to make my car payments and pay for the insurance coverage.

I began my career in the pediatric unit and worked every other weekend in the newborn nursery. I slowly developed a desire to become a pediatric nurse practitioner. I was fortunate to work with some wonderful nurse practitioners and pediatricians who were very supportive of my goal. I was a dreamer. Before I left that healthcare setting as an LPN I had worked on an orthopedic unit and also found it to be very interesting and fulfilling. But, it wasn't my passion.

I graduated from practical nursing school in June, and immediately found the employment I needed. Employment opportunities immediately following nursing school graduation are not much different today. The need remains high, especially for registered nurses. Just find your area of interest and go for it. Unlike in years past when you were told you needed two years of medical-surgical nursing before entering a specialty area, today just go where you believe you will be happy. Why work where you are unhappy from your first day?

The girl from high school and I were still seeing each other and not long after graduation I presented her with a diamond. It was October 6th at a quarter to six. She had just graduated high school in June. I asked her to marry me at The View; a place near home for romantic evenings. I probably would not be able to find the place today, but I do have a few stories from that place. Her first words, before she gave a response to the

59

question I had asked, were, "Take me to see my mother." Eventually she did respond with a yes. It was special for me that my grandmother accompanied me on the trip picking out the engagement ring and the wedding set.

I had a job and so did my girl from high school. It was time for us to settle down. After all, I was at her apartment more than I was at home. She didn't have a vehicle, so I provided her rides to and from work and school. She had already registered into a local community college nursing program.

So much for moving forward to school! Wedding bells were ringing. Some years later we did register at the same local community college in the liberal arts and science courses, to become registered nurses. Her grandmother stipulated that she complete her RN before we got a wedding gift. The stipulation remained in effect and my wife lived up to it many years later. We didn't think so at the time but her grandmother was a wise, wise woman; what the hell were we thinking anyway? We were a couple of crazy kids; hardly past nineteen. Our parents had to sign for the wedding to become operative.

During working as an LPN I developed a desire to be an RN and not only an RN but to achieve my dream of being a pediatric nurse practitioner. I worked when I could with both a pediatrician and pediatric nurse practitioner. They were nice enough to take me under their wings, but I was nowhere near ready to fly. Remember, I was an LPN and had a great deal of education ahead of me. I knew someday I was going to be at the top in my nursing career.

Funny thing is today I'd like to be a mental health nurse practitioner and work with young people facing adversities. See how things change? I had no interest in mental health years ago, and now it greatly interests me. Adversities made me a better nursing professor. See how your dreams transform. I was a dreamer. With marriage in sight the whole pediatric-nurse-practitioner thing would simply fade into my history. Programs were not as accessible as they are today. It would've required moving to a city in the middle of the state and I certainly wouldn't have been able to work. That light was thinning out. Now, I am simply too old for this dream, but I was guided to my calling.

"Never give up on a dream just because of the time it will take to accomplish it.

The time will pass anyway."

Earl Nightingale

As time progressed, we completed our liberal arts and science courses at the local community college. Many nurses with an LPN talked about the Regents External Degree program while we worked together. That institute became Regents College later, Excelsior College later still, and today is Excelsior University. We had been practicing LPNs for over three years. This program was something we could do at our own pace together. We embarked on our journey with two friends sharing an interest in an RN degree through the Regents External Degree program. Our dedication spurred, we pushed forward with a weekly study group schedule. Study guides provided us with a format before a written exam, while a successful score guaranteed completion of each of the nursing program's areas, such as fundamentals, behavioral health, maternal and child. We took the written exams on a local university campus an hour away. Everyone was excited about this educational journey. The thought of being RNs at our current place of employment was a primary motivating factor. You see, at some point we all shared a similar career goal and dream.

With time, other study group members dropped out of the program. I completed all written exams. Now it was time for the clinical performance exam. I was one step from graduation and becoming eligible to take the State Board of Nursing RN exam. These were days before the current NCLEX-RN exams and computer testing. The State Board of Nursing RN exams required sitting in a convention hall and coloring in scantron dots for two days. I was a dreamer and kept the vision in the light until I could see an end in sight. I will discuss this part of my educational journey in a later chapter.

"I can do all this through him who gives me strength"

Philippians 4:13

Life had come a long way. Traveling somewhere, we purchased a clock, our names etched on it and a larger-than-life "RN" showing in the center. Still displayed in our home office today, it was our incentive never to stop moving. Think about buying yourself an incentive gift that motivates you to keep moving forward.

After I became an academic, I handled the dread students experienced toward the end of the semester by having them hang their commencement regalia. I told them to choose a visible place inside their homes that wouldn't allow them to steal their gaze.

Knowing they would walk across that stage on graduation day motivated them. And they did walk! It made for some remarkably experienced outcomes.

Don't be afraid; Just Believe

Mark 5:36

I apologize for straying from my journey to RN. We routinely skimmed the Help Wanted ads in the local paper during this period. We could find something that could enhance our incomes. During one of the reviews, I noticed an ad wanting a camp nurse. Since both of us had volunteered in the past to bring home developmentally disabled children, we thought we should give the number a call. It would provide us with an increase in our income during the summer, and it would be fun.

So, I called, and the gentleman on the other end invited me for an interview. He gave me the directions, and we drove, and drove, and drove. At one point, I decided we would round one more curve in the road, and if the camp wasn't there, we would head back home.

Neither of us had any idea where we were heading. The road at times was as rough as a washboard, and it seemed to go nowhere. We began to believe someone had put a prank ad in the paper to have people drive into nowhere.

"No eye has seen, no ear has heard, and no mind has imagined what God has prepared for those who love him."

1 Corinthians 2:9 (NLT)

We rounded another curve and finally saw the sign for the scout reservation. I went to the door alone, and a lovely gentleman answered the door. He introduced himself and said I could bring my "friend" in. I explained it was my wife. He instructed me to get her, and we entered his home. He asked if we drank coffee. We acknowledged that we drank coffee, and then he asked permission to smoke. At the time, both of us were smokers. (I am happy to admit we have been smoking-free for many years.) He seemed delighted. I was married, drank coffee, and smoked. He also was able to secure two nurses for the price of one.

Our next eight years with him, his wife, his family, and the camp staff were some of the most beautiful years of our lives. We loved the area so much that we began to look for property. We were going to build our dream

65

home there someday. I had done some substitute school nursing and knew we didn't want our children to go to a city school after a student bent over, lifted her skirt, and told me to kiss her ass. When I reported this to the administration, they did zilch — time to look for a better school district for our future children. So, the dream continued.

As most young couples, we wanted children. That was to be a long, disappointing road. Adversity struck once again. After much testing, we discovered we would not have children. Another adversity and the worst, so I believed. Remember, always remember where you came from.

Adoption was most certainly the answer, so with the help of my urologist we contacted the local county social services office and completed the application and interview process. We were approved. Paperwork and home visit complete.

We waited and waited and continued to dream. Days turned to weeks, weeks to months, and months to a year. On a sunny Friday afternoon in September, we received a phone call from our caseworker who asked if we would be interested in a baby boy. She went through a laundry list of "would you take a baby if questions." She later arrived at our home with a picture of the perfect baby boy you have ever seen. He had the most beautiful long eyelashes and was excellent. All the "what if" questions she asked didn't matter. It was love at first sight. They informed us on that sunny Friday we would be parents on Monday afternoon. We had nothing. No crib, no diapers, no clothing, no food, not a thing for a baby.

"Therefore, I say to you, do not worry about your life, what you will eat or what you will drink; nor about your body, what you will put on. Is not life more than food and the body more than clothing? Look at the birds of the air, for they neither sow nor reap nor gather into barns, yet your heavenly Father feeds them. Are you not of more value than they?"

Matthew 6:25-26 (NKJV)

Everything had to be perfect by Monday. After all, I am a dreamer. We did have a credit card and went shopping. Boy, did we go shopping. Our son arrived and had the perfect baby's room. Our families would later give us a baby shower and our new family of three lacked nothing. As sure as the sun shines, this child was loved. He shares the bond of never forgetting where you come from with me.

Within his first three years we would sell our home in the city and build our dream home in the hills. He would go to Boy Scout summer camp with us and became the camp kid. We knew if he wasn't with us, he was with a scout troop, and he was always ready for bed by night. He was the most beautiful child you can imagine. He still is a very handsome man today. Just ask his mother and wife. Of course, dad thinks so too. Our adversities became a tremendous success that continues today.

The camp director introduced us to the local real estate agent, helping us search for a property. We had been looking at log home models and fell in love with a rustic version. Of course, we had our home in a nearby community, but I was the dreamer. We put the house on the market and sold it within one week. There had been a flood in a nearby community north of us. People lost their homes. The sale was rapid and we were left essentially homeless. However, we gained a great property in a beautiful hilly country setting.

The camp director saved the day by allowing us to store our furniture in one of the camp buildings while our home was being built. I was the dreamer, and we would have our beautiful new home, just like the model home we had picked out. The timing couldn't have been any more perfect. The new log home would be ready at the end of the summer camp season, and we would be able to move in at the close of camp. But that was not going to be the case. We are going to see why in Slip ups & Trip ups.

So, the dreamer has graduated high school and nursing school. He has purchased a new car, become gainfully employed and gotten married. Closer than ever to completing an associate of science degree in nursing, he has sold a home and purchased land for a dream home. He received the most precious gift of a child when it was impossible to do it on his own.

It has to be our faith not only in ourselves but also in our God. The confidence that everything will work out and be wonderful; the belief that God would provide in his time (this will be tested again and again), and a faith that it is terrific for dreamers to dream. This didn't stop the *why* questions from happening. It was wonderful, but it could not have happened without climbing hills, crossing rivers and traversing dark valleys.

I have fought the good fight, I have finished the race, I have kept the faith.

2 Timothy 4:7

Now, after hearing all I said you won't catch me saying I never went through a dark hour. Some of you are probably going to be shocked. I once came to believe suicide was best. That was when the pain got heavier than shovels gashing the earth. Taking the easy way out of the pain proposed itself as the only solution because I wanted to run away from everything. There had to be a better place for me somewhere. Heaven was a beautiful place without pain, wasn't it? Anyplace but where I was must be better, I thought. And so, I experienced times when I truly thought I should prefer death to continuing with the adversity I faced. The grave was better than coming to terms with it. I have asked myself "Why?" many times. I know now I am worth so much more. Bumps in the road got a little bigger than usual, that's all.

"My life is worth the living, I don't need to see the end."

John Denver's Sweet Surrender

Have you ever wondered that the 'why' question is the most tormenting thought that

70

haunts us during such a dark hour? We don't rebel against the overwhelming emotion so much as wanting to know why. Why am I going through this?

When adversity looks us in the face we are forced to tackle it. The more we tackle it and finally overthrow it, the more we relish the comfort that follows the distress. Maybe this is why I can understand so well the struggle of unsuccessful students today.

"Why is this happening to me"; — isn't that what you keep saying to yourself?

If you are new at having a spiritual belief you may believe it is unreasonable for bad things to happen to you. As you mature you will realize you learn from these situations. Sometimes, many years later the 'why' question will be turned into 'Oh, now I know why'. Many of my adversities brought me to where I am today, and it really isn't too bad a place to be.

If you are in a similar place today, I will immediately ask you this:

Put down this book and call for help.

Seek out someone you can talk to.

Pick up your cell phone and **Dial 988 Suicide and Crisis Lifeline**.

Remember, you matter to others. Get the help you need. Be selfish in this situation and rid yourself of your demons. Suicide is not the solution. It will only transfer your pain to those who love you.

I implore you to make the call if you are feeling this way. **Dial 988!**

I continue to have the necessary people in my life. It's what keeps me from getting into a rut. I used to lack the plan and the resources. There were nights I went to bed praying to God to flush the thoughts away from my head. Then I looked at pictures of my family and knew they were my light.

Following the death of my mother, there were days I believed being with her would have been better than the pain. I made myself think being with her was the only place I wanted to be. Emptiness lived in me for a long time.

Then I grabbed myself by the bootstraps and contacted a counselor. Perhaps you are feeling this way now. Remember you are not alone. Love must come from within. We need to love ourselves before we can love anyone else.

Counseling can help you make that connection.

I'm glad I got up off my haunches to seek out a counselor. I have access to him even today. It helps! We can all use a therapist from time to time. It's nothing to be ashamed of and I believe it is the intelligent thing to do. It is someone who will just walk the path with you and who isn't intimately involved in your life. Sometimes you need someone from the outside to tell you that you are okay. It is someone who can see the forest without getting caught up in the trees.

I understand counseling can be expensive. Your local church has someone who is qualified to help you initially on a road to recovery. Seek out a professional, whether it is a pastor, priest, rabbi, or any clergy. They can give you direction and perhaps assist in meeting any financial need. You are important enough to start taking advantage of any available resources. I know I mattered and so do you.

Listen to counsel and receive instruction so that you may be wise later in life.

Proverbs 19:20

73

I don't believe God is done with me yet. I know you have someone in your life who feels the same about you.

*But **everything exposed by the light becomes visible and everything that is illuminated becomes a light**.*

Ephesians 5:13

The emphasis is on grace. The power of faith, sometimes shrunk to the size of a mustard seed, but holding on nonetheless, brought out the dreamer in me. In all of this I have always remembered where I came from. Keep the focus on your calling and maintain faith in yourself. You will endure no matter what adversities fall in your path. You will retain guidance through the bleakest hardship if you truly follow your calling.

"We can cultivate a dream for our lives that outlasts the world, transforms time, changes eternity, and advances His cause and His Kingdom for His glory!"

David Jeremiah

VI

Because We Could

Love is patient, love is kind. It does not envy, it does not boast, it is not proud. It does not dishonor others, it is not self-seeking, it is not easily angered, it keeps no record of wrongs. Love does not delight in evil but rejoices with the truth. It always protects, always trusts, always hopes, always perseveres.

1 CORINTHIANS 13:4-7

We were only nineteen at the time we married. Did I hear someone say too young to tie the knot? We were in love. We were soul mates and partners in crime. We were dreamers with big dreams.

My parents were skeptical as I suspected they would be. Apparently, discussions took place between them and her mom. But, no one was going to stand in our way. We weren't aware of what was said in any of those discussions but we knew if we fell on our faces, we would have to get back up and start again.

The wedding took place shortly after nursing graduation, in January 1979, much to the dismay of her grandmother. Those were times when the younger you were married, the better we believed it to be.

If she hadn't been in love with me and I hadn't been full of myself, I suspect we might have listened to her grandmother. We might have waited a little longer to be with each other but that did not figure in our life-plan. As usual, hindsight is always twenty-twenty.

After attending a friend's wedding we rescheduled our date to the month following it. That left us with thirty days to plan our wedding. Our initial plan was to wait for spring, but I'm not sure we ever intended on waiting until we both were RNs. Somehow, I don't believe the outcome would have been the same had we waited.

Then the rumors started: people talking she had to be pregnant for us to be rushing it; that her grandparents were not attending the wedding, etc.

Well, in the days leading up to the ceremony, we did suspect her grandmother was not going to attend neither was she going to allow her grandfather to do so. In the end, they came to the wedding.

But a wedding gift would not be in the offing until I graduated from RN school in 1983. At that point we had been married four years without children.

We received half the gift as promised following my graduation. It wouldn't be until thirty-one years later the other half of the gift would be given. Even in death I believe her grandmother kept her word, and I believe it was given when my wife was in her final semester of RN school. Her grandmother was a wise, wise woman.

The wedding was conducted according to Catholic statutes, even though I was brought up a Dutch Reformed Protestant. I would not change my religious affiliation until several years later and after our children had arrived.

*For example, by law **a married woman is bound to her husband as long as he is alive**, but if her husband dies, she is released from the law that binds her to him.*

Romans 7:2

We learned over time that many of our classmates' marriages didn't last. I know ours had the grace of God and lots of hard work behind it.

I'm sure it is a divine intervention that keeps us together and moving forward. If you don't have faith in yourself and in God watching over your marriage, I have no idea how it will survive.

Even with God's help at your side, there arise many times of adversity and hours of darkness. Somehow our light keeps glowing.

We promised to stay together through good times and bad and we did it because we could. We experienced the best of the best and the worst of the worst. But I have never forgotten where I came from.

*She shall continue to be his wife; **he must not divorce her as long as he lives**.*

Deuteronomy 22:19

"That is why a man leaves his father and mother and is united to his wife, and they become one flesh."

Genesis 2:24 (NIV)

As I look back at the first month of 1979, I wonder if it was an escape. For me, it might have been an escape from the years of

78

taunting and the slew of hurtful names. Perhaps an escape from not being anyone? Or for her an escape from a disruptive family life? The status of being married unfolds a larger social network before us, after all.

At the same time, I certainly could use this opportunity to escape my past experiences. Leaving the torment of my youth behind me, I could become a responsible adult. It was a means of gaining greater control over my future. The two of us could create a stable household together.

But time shows us that contrary to the perspective we have as young people, we don't have control over anything. Yes, being a married young man meant no more questions from anyone. Now, I was going to be on my own and be free.

My thoughts at the time were no different from most thoughts harbored by young people today. After raising wonderful sons, I know they too thought the same things. All they wanted was out of the house.

And yet, nothing can replace the joys my wife and I experienced raising a family together.

"One of the keys to going forward according to God's design is being able to determine the one most important thing in your life."

David Jeremiah

We were happy in our one-bedroom apartment, sleeping in a twin bed, and watching a black-and-white 13-inch television with aluminum foil on the rabbit ears. We wouldn't have cable until later.

We stayed in that apartment until returning home one evening after work and discovered one of her younger brothers sitting on the outside steps in a snowstorm. We had planned to go skiing the next morning. The landlady heard him upstairs and kicked him out. We didn't have any restriction of overnight guests in our rental agreement. We also discovered that the landlord had been going through our apartment behind our back. Then we found a cable bill with our name on it which was actually the landlady's cable bill. So she was trying to dupe us. We didn't go skiing the next day. Instead, we called some friends, packed up a few pickup trucks and relocated to a two-bedroom apartment back home. We were able to overcome the adversity.

There is a funny incident I'd like to include at this point. I always relate it whenever anyone asks me how long she and I have been together. We met in kindergarten, seemingly, under circumstances that were not so pleasant.

I travel back in time to that kindergarten class where I am sitting in a swing and this kindergarten girl is waiting impatiently for her turn. Well, I don't recall this specific incident and she and I did not have the same kindergarten teacher. She says it happened although I still am not convinced it did. Apparently, I had been on the swing too long, and her patience was running out faster than a dog will lick a dish clean. So she walked up and pushed me off. Now, that probably contributes to my lack of recall. I should have known better then.

She has always provided the following rationale for why she did it: she was brought up with five brothers and had to defend herself. I am still not sure how pushing a harmless little fellow off the swing could count as defending yourself against anything other than the fact that she wanted the swing all to herself.

The story brings lots of laughter and I suspect we've been together in some way or other since that first fall. This is just another example of how different lives are brought together, and we find the support to overcome future adversities.

This girl from high school who would later become my wife came from a home with five brothers and her mom. Her father unfortunately had been out of the picture for years. It was an adversity that she overcame. With the support of her grandparents, she was raised along with brothers in a stable environment.

Her father appeared later after we were married and created a small amount of turmoil, but all ended well. Even through his adversities, his daughter cared for him. By all accounts, her childhood years may not have been the greatest.

My home and family were a bit more of a 'home' to her. I believe my family was more secure in its ties among the members. We also enjoyed what may be identified as better opportunities by some.

I remember a family vacation in the spring of 1977 prior to my high school graduation. Since I would be off to school or maybe work soon after, mom and dad didn't agree on having that girl along as it probably was going to be my last vacation with my sister and parents. The girl was fine with that, she always understood. My return home from a family vacation would always be cause for celebration between me and that girl from high school who later became my wife.

I generally returned with some small token of love like a stuffed bear or some souvenir from where I had been. When she spent the weekends at my house, she slept in my sister's room. We were respectable church-going family. It was simply not allowed for teenagers of the opposite gender to sleep together. I don't believe it damaged either of us and at the time it was certainly the right thing to do. I may have asked her to sneak in during the night, but she certainly didn't want to be discovered and disappoint my mom and dad. So we kept our distance.

My household provided me with nothing less than a great life but I felt it was over-controlling at times. Well, what teenage doesn't think that? So, the opportunity to be at her house for me was a bit of a freeing experience, so to speak.

It was dramatically more relaxed. This type of environment was a drawing card not only for me, but many young people within the community. Not that it was totally out of control—at least most of the time, but it was relaxed. Certainly, more relaxed than being home.

My future brothers-in-law would come to my house to play poker with my mom. Some of those quarter games had high stakes. They spent many a wonderful evening playing cards.

At their home, it was not unlikely to see 10 to 12 individuals (adults and teens) at the kitchen table on any given night. With six kids, if each brought home one friend you had a dozen for dinner. Weekends were a 'free-for-all'.

My mother-in-law cooked for dozens but is not cooking much any longer. She was an amazing cook. Her home-cooked spaghetti, meatballs, and sausage along with goulash were a community favorite. The large pot sat on the stove, and it wasn't uncommon to grab a fork and get yourself a meatball as you passed the stove. Sometimes her meals traveled to other communities and fed several families. Those were some wonderful days. Her mother always went above and beyond to provide for the seven of them and anyone else who may have wandered in. If her mom had to work two or three jobs to make ends meet, she did not flinch from doing it. This woman was never a selfish individual and she never took away from her children.

Time kept moving and we spent hours together during the last couple of years in high school. I remember one junior year Halloween, when I lost my class ring while I was out during the evening after having received it a few days before. A group of us, who became friends (I wasn't alone any longer), had been indulging in mischief. We had playing those old-fashioned Halloween pranks. No property damage, just lots of fun (involving lots of toilet paper and shaving cream, you know?).

I knew the general area where I'd dropped it, but it was impossible to find it at night. The next morning, that girl (who loves me and has always done anything and everything to make me happy) rode a bike (it may have been mine) two miles from her house to mine. She met an accident on the bridge she had to cross to get to my house. It did some damage to her knees, but she searched and found my class ring. I still have that ring today. I should have recognized then it was love.

"And when she finds it, she calls her friends and neighbors together and says, 'Rejoice with me; I have found my lost coin.'

Luke 15:9

Our families celebrated holidays together and my parents always treated her, her brothers, mother and extended family as part of our family. We never had complaints on how we had been treated by her family. I had found another dreamer and it was wonderful. She had a difficult childhood, and her dreams of white picket fences were just as real as mine. We were the best of friends in the best of times. In time we'd become soul mates in the worst of times.

God sets the lonely in families, he leads out the prisoners with singing;

Psalm 68:6

We moved ahead with the wedding with her oldest brother filling in the role of best man. He stepped into what should have been her dad's role in walking her down the aisle. It was different from the start. As he walked her toward me in this huge church, she was the most beautiful bride in the whole world.

Every bride is a princess and that day I saw mine. Probably I took that for granted at the time as well. No doubt I did. The wedding was just as we wanted and took place without any issues. It was beautiful. Everyone believes their wedding is the most beautiful. Looking back, I know ours was.

Standing in front of the church, I really had no idea what I was doing. I knew she was sure of what she was doing. After all, we were just kids. We were always told as children that girls mature faster than boys and now, I was certain of that. We had attended the meetings with her parish priest, but they were nothing like they are today. We moved forward and made a life for ourselves, and boy have we made it.

We have kept going through the good times and bad, sickness and health. The till death do us part has been a serious phrase during our life together.

You don't need to allow your past to drive your future. You can overcome and advance forward. Perhaps in sharing some of this your adversities won't seem so big. Through what I have shared I hope you can see my past didn't determine my future. And the same can be true for you.

VII

Family

He must manage his own family well and see that his children obey him, and he must do so in a manner worthy of full respect.

1 Timothy 3:4

One day I was part of a family of four and the next day it was a family of eleven! Time rode on a chariot of the wind. Our extended families were even larger and have grown substantially over the years. I hailed from a family structure that in many respects was starkly different. They say opposites attract. Maybe they do, but they certainly don't do it peacefully.

The differences have helped us grow. I was not born with a silver spoon, but I wanted to provide one for my family and so did she. There continue to be times, when being *opposite* becomes opposition on a large scale.

88

It is an adversity we both continue to overcome. Even as I write this book, the grains of sand help my pearl develop; and I'm certain the grains are doing the same for her pearl.

Allow me to explain what I am talking about. The formation of a pearl begins when a foreign substance (sand) slips into the oyster and causes irritation. The oyster secretes a mineral substance that coats the grain of sand, until the pearl is formed. I work every day and so do you, on creating a pearl.

Somehow opposites do attract, but at times it shatters the peace. You learn to cope and be tolerant. Just as grains of sand in an oyster will produce a pearl, so do the frustrations that come with being opposites. She and I are working on developing a pearl together every day. This is what keeps the relationship interesting. These difficulties make you grow.

We make every attempt to keep God front and center. This isn't always easy, but we share the satisfaction of living up to our belief. This really continues to be the foundation of how we succeed. It can be twisted and discussed in several ways, but it is only by the grace of God that we will truly live out our promise: till death do us part.

89

I am fortunate to have a believing soul mate. We share the values and perspectives of believers. You must notice my faith has been a saving grace through many of my dark times. It matters to me, and it matters to us. Perhaps, in time it will matter to you.

*For kings and all those in authority, that **we may live peaceful and quiet lives** in all godliness and holiness.*

1 Timothy 2:2

*May your fountain be blessed, and may you rejoice in the **wife of your youth**.*

Proverbs 5:18

My parents and her mom were always very supportive of us. They would go above and beyond during the hard times to help us make ends meet. I recall one Christmas when we were given an immense box full of diapers, baby food, toilet paper, paper towels, and a variety of items necessary for the home and a baby. It was one of the best gifts we ever received. It did get tough sometimes. We had purchased a home, had a car payment, and home expenses while each of us made $3.75 an hour as LPNs.

We were making a combined salary of over fifteen thousand dollars annually and we were king and queen of our castle. We seemed to have enough most of the time yet there were days we worried about where the groceries would come from or where we'd get the money to pay the utilities. We settled for many of the things that could be given to us and really didn't have a worry in the world. Hand-me-downs were wonderful. Times were rough, and we never forgot where we came from.

"Therefore, I tell you, do not worry about your life, what you will eat or drink; or about your body, what you will wear. Is not life more than food, and the body more than clothes? Look at the birds of the air; they do not sow or reap or store away in barns, and yet your heavenly Father feeds them. Are you not much more valuable than they? Can any one of you by worrying add a single hour to your life?"

Matthew 6:25-27

One thing was certain. We both never ignored the importance of family, faith and a reliance on our God. Not to say our family was uncomplicated or without distractions, distresses and adversities. But at the end of every day, family was important, and the foundation of our relationship had to be cemented on our belief in a God. As with any

91

family we have watched it grow, shared in the joys, and suffered through the disappointments. We have lost loved ones and shared in the joy of adoptions and births. We have never forgotten where we came from.

Importance of family is irrevocable. I wanted to share this with you as an avenue for you to find your strength when you believe your possibilities are limited.

Family, not necessarily the bond of blood, but the bond of love and caring can be important when you think you are at the end of your rope. Remember, I started without a family? Remember, I was alone? I was drawn to the open hearts of my parents and later to another family many would consider broken. Funny thing is that's where I found the greatest bonds of love.

Sometimes I think I was meant to save the day. Now I know my arrival was welcomed into a home filled with love. It was in each other's presence that they found the motivation to keep moving.

How wonderful it is to see that life for them sustained the shakes of fortune down the years. No matter what life threw at them, they held on to the trust emanating from being a family. In many respects, that broken home was not much different than my own. Once you move past the fear, there is love, and plenty of it. Love endures all things.

Therefore, we will not fear, though the earth gives way and the mountains fall into the heart of the sea,

Psalm 46:2

We were young dreamers with families. What's more? We were the first to embark on a college education. Neither of my parents was able to complete high school. Dad went off to serve in the Second World War, whereas mom made it to the twelfth grade only to drop out when she lost interest in the whole school idea after she was unsuccessful at shorthand, or so she said.

I suspect times were bleak and mom went to work to help support her family. Dad sent his military pay home for his mom to use and supported his younger siblings. Dad's father passed away at a very young age, so dad went off to the war to support those who remained back home. My adversities can't compare to the complications that lay across their path.

Following the death of my father, we were able to have a high school diploma awarded to him posthumously since he had left school to serve as a soldier. It was a proud day for mom as she accepted his diploma. Coincidently, they awarded dad's diploma in the same ceremony that graduated one of his great nephews. Not planned, but a nice surprise. I keep his diploma safe even today. I will discuss the loss of my dad later. Another walk through a dark time that made me stronger, resulting in other successes. Through adversities, life continued.

My wife and I started our young family. Our oldest arrived in September of 1982. He was born in June and on a beautiful Monday afternoon in September we were given our beautiful baby boy in a conference room at a county social services office in a nearby city.

Five years later, our youngest son would arrive early in the morning on a hot July day. Five years earlier we had not been able to have children and on July 31st, 1987, our second son came into the world. It was God's blessed work and intervention. I had a subsequent conversation with my urologist (who was a wonderful practitioner) about the test that said we couldn't have children. His response: "Well Russ, it only takes one." We still laugh about that today.

Although the boys arrived in totally different ways, each delivery was special and a time of unlimited love. Both sons were welcomed into our families and have been loved every day since. Today they are truly brothers and once again it is not the blood that binds us. An adversity turned into wonderful success.

Nursing infants gurgle choruses about you; toddlers shout the songs That drown out enemy talk, and silence atheist babble.

Psalm 8:2 (MSG)

One of my brothers-in-law would pass suddenly and unexpectedly on a cold November morning in 1997. He had just returned from hunting and was enjoying a second cup of coffee and interestingly a conversation about heaven with a mutual family friend.

I will never forget that call from my youngest brother-in-law. There are no words to describe how you feel when you get a call that your brother-in-law is dead. I was immediately challenged on how to relay the message to his sister and his two young nephews. I was in shock and still had to carry out the responsibility of telling everyone in my family.

It was a difficult time (he was in his mid-thirties), but as a family we moved forward and cherished the wonderful memories we have of him. His favorite blanket remains in my car today. Once again, it is only by the hands of God, love of each other and family that kept us moving forward.

Several years later we would convert our two-car garage into a mother-in-law apartment and each time I tried to hang my brother-in-law's picture it would fall. After three attempts I asked my mother-in-law to hang the picture. It hasn't fallen!

"I will deliver these people from the power of the grave; I will redeem them from death. Where, O death, are your plagues? Where, O grave, is your destruction?

Hosea 13:14 (NIV)

What does all this have to do with you? How can knowing this help you in your adversity? Turn back a page or two. This chapter is "family." I could change it to "Support" or "Advocacy." I am sure it will become much clearer as you continue this journey with me.

To move from our darkness, our disappointments, death, and the "slip ups or trip ups," "into the light" and on to our

96

successes, we need support. Support of our family, significant others, teacher, professor, pastor, or a foundation in faith that can provide us with strength to move forward.

Through love, support, family, and faith anything is possible. The dreamer can dream, the loner can find love, and the underachiever can reach the summit.

"Faith is to believe what we do not see; and the reward of this faith is to see what we believe."

-Augustine

VIII

Slip ups, Trip ups

It was when I found out I could make mistakes that I knew I was on to something.

Ornette Coleman

Everyone falls at some point, right? You've got to. Otherwise, how'd you learn to handle yourself in an unfavorable situation? If you want to be a climber, you will have to put your faith to the test. That next adversity might be waiting round the corner. It would only serve your true interest if you strap up and get ready.

At first I could not choose between "Mistakes & Failures" and "Slip ups or Trip ups" to be the title of this chapter. You can see what my decision was, now.

No one likes to make a mistake and I don't think anyone wants to be a failure. But we have disappointments, setbacks, and delayed opportunities. Dark moments don't make me a failure, and neither do they make you one. The perspective we build regarding events or situations determine the emotions we associate with those events. And it can make all the difference to the outcome in life.

What is failure? It is a *lack of success*. Allow yourself a positive attitude to lead your life.

Here's the craziest crash course in the world in Perspective.

If you opened your eyes and were able to get out of bed this morning, you were successful.

If you were unable to get out of bed but opened your eyes, you were successful.

When you are unable to get out of bed or open your eyes, you are successful, because you're alive.

If your heart continues to beat, you have the opportunity to be successful.

You have the potential for future success through finding your purpose.

Someone needs you.

A perspective doesn't need to be defined so much as it needs to be lived. Live a new perspective from scratch and let it be your guide.

Let's have look at it another way.

I must retake the exam because "I am a failure." See? Why not say: You experienced a setback and will pass the exam on your next attempt? Why not say: You'll work harder, get help, and pass the next exam?

You were unsuccessful, but that was only your first attempt. Why pull yourself back from the possibility you'll do better with the next attempt? No one's paying you to make yourself think you won't, are they? No one's charging you for making yourself think you will, either. Pay yourself some positivity.

No one ever led a life without its share of negative moments. No roulette was born for you to place your bet on a slot and win each time. You will lose, and the negative gene will get to you. There's no point seeing the world through rose-tinted shades. But I bet I want to be as positive about life as I possibly can for as long as I'm around. At some point you just must pick yourself up, brush yourself off and keep moving forward. Shit will happen, but we mustn't let it destroy us. There are better things for us ahead if we keep our faith.

But are you ready to embrace the darkness before you can turn on the light? And how do you embrace that darkness, when it is precisely what you must aim to conquer? It is during the time of darkness when our faith should be strong or at least be somewhat evident. If not a faith in God, then most certainly start with faith in yourself because it's essential you believe in yourself. That is resource no. 1 for you right there.

And then, try having a little faith in God and see where it takes you. That does not translate into becoming a devout Christian so much as it means that you allow yourself the realization that there are things you cannot control. When you ease yourself into that realization, you learn to forgive yourself for the events you could never have helped.

After all, if we were really in charge would we allow these things to happen? If I was in charge, would I have chosen to be an orphan? I am thankful that the woman who gave me life did not choose abortion.

Things may not turn out according to what we have in mind. Acknowledgement of life being planned leads each moment of darkness to become an opportunity of trying to imagine the "bigger picture." However you may define it, but we need faith. We need to believe the "big plan", the "big picture"; the "big dream." Perhaps, we as a society have trivialized this outreach of the human heart by mowing it down to reward and punishment.

The least of you will become a thousand, the smallest a mighty nation. I am the Lord; in its time I will do this swiftly."

Isaiah 60:22 (NIV)

The runt will become a great tribe, the weakling become a strong nation. I am God. At the right time I'll make it happen."

Isaiah 60:22 (MSG)

Look at me. Did I always have this kind of faith? I must respond with an honest, resounding and affirming, no.

There are still days when I question everything. I question my life, my profession, decisions I took five years ago. I pore incessantly over my reasons for thinking I'm happy with my life. Believe me, the "why" questions haven't lost the habit of coming back to gnaw at the back of my mind.

I most certainly experienced doubt in my faith at the end of my associate nursing degree program when I believe I may have completely lost my faith in myself and God. I began to believe nursing was not my vocation. This period for me was indeed a dark time. The experience was unquestionably one of the worst adversities in my life. I was nothing but a failure, was the belief that ran deepest in me; that I was never going to complete my registered nursing degree and would remain an LPN for my career. Not a bad thing, but it wasn't my goal because I had a dream.

Perhaps some readers have had a similar experience and can relate to this. Some of you may have experienced something just as traumatic or worse and haven't dealt with it still. I suspect many nursing students will be able to relate and perhaps some nursing faculty (if they are honest) will as well.

Nursing students, if you have experienced a monitored simulation, skills' lab, or clinical experience, you will totally understand. I had completed all of the written exams for my degree in associate nursing. Well, this was the next and the final step in completing all requirements for receiving a university degree. I would be the first in my family to complete high school and college. This was not only a major accomplishment for me, but also my family.

The clinical performance in a nursing exam. It doesn't only sound a bit ominous; it was ominous. At the time I was an LPN with several years of nursing experience. I completed the practice for the performance exam during my scheduled shifts under the supervision of an RN who had completed the same program. We both felt I was ready for the exam.

This competency exam is administered over two-and-a-half days. It begins on a Friday evening with a lab, ending on Sunday afternoon or evening depending on the candidate's success. The cost of the exam (at the time) was seven hundred, fifty dollars; today this exam is over one thousand dollars. You must successfully complete all aspects of care for the patient assigned, including a nursing care plan.

Friday evening's experience begins in a lab setting and the proctor monitors the candidate while they perform several nursing skills. The evening passed. Saturday brought on the actual patient assignments. To complete the exam the candidate must successfully provide care for two adult and one pediatric patient.

The specifics aren't relevant at this point. What I will share is I never repeated those errors. The outcome was "failure" and documented as "unsuccessful." You see if you "never forget where you came from," it will give you a better perspective on where you are today. I absolutely gained an understanding of walking in a nursing student's shoes.

My world ended at that time and I was in a world without a God watching over it. Why, why, why? I didn't make the cut because He had left me on my own. I was being run over by a rampage of "why" questions. But God can bring good from any dark and I felt His artistry at work while I was going through the internal torture.

I realized the emphasis in my "why" questions was in the wrong places. He didn't turn His back, but what I wanted wasn't in His time yet. I never made those errors again and neither have my students. That's what was important to learn for the safety of my patients. If you "never forget where you came from" it will make you a better person, nurse, and mentor.

Consider it nothing but joy, my brothers, and sisters, whenever you fall into various trials. Be assured that the testing of your faith

105

(through experience) produces endurance (leading to spiritual maturity, and inner peace).

(Trials: These are outward circumstances, conflicts, sufferings, and troubles encountered by all believers).

James 1:2-4 (AMP)

My dark time was my test. My failure was my trial. I was unsuccessful because I wasn't ready, and God knew it. Apparently so did the examiner.

Some months later I scheduled and retested. This experience would also be a rapid weight loss program for me. During the next attempt I managed to lose fifteen pounds over the two-and-a-half days the practical exam was administered. I learned where the chapel was in the hospital the exam was administered in, and spent every moment there in prayer when I wasn't assigned at the bedside. Perhaps that is what was missing the first time.

During this experience, every patient was an orthopedic patient, and that just happened to be where I was and had been working as an LPN. This experience is so clear to me now. At the time, who should I have blamed? Why? Obtaining my college degree this way left a very large void where I should have a mentor or advocate who was associated with the program. I truly was alone but, I never forgot where I came from.

This experience helped develop my nursing practice and made me a better nurse, and a nursing professor. Subsequent educational experiences would provide the necessary support to forward me through my academic journey. My mentor in my doctorate program was amazing. She knew when something was amiss and provided immediate intervention, advocacy, and support. I am fortunate we are colleagues and friends today and her guidance is still greatly appreciated.

If you currently do not believe you have any form of "faith", I assure you, you do. I have seen more "OMGs" in text messages than I could ever count. Try believing them, because when you call, He listens.

Please don't misunderstand. I am not telling you to do nothing and to sit-back in your easy chair and see what life has in store for you. I can assure you, the rent or mortgage may not get paid, the lights could be shut off, and you will be in a much darker place. Sometimes the dark places we experience make us better, and we must always keep moving forward until we can look back and never forget where we came from.

This is the message we have heard from him and declare to you: God is light; in him there is no darkness at all.

1 John 1:5 (NIV)

Navigating the path of adversity, we may not think that is true. The waterfall of the "why" questions is plunging you down. Why did He do this to me? Why is He making me go through this? What did I do to deserve this?

Fortunately for me, from infancy to adulthood I had loving parents, grandparents, and a loving family. But I will admit there were times when I would run through my waterfall and simply say: God doesn't exist.

I was raised in a "religion" and today it is evident I need a "relationship" with the God I have faith in. The older I get the more real this becomes. As I look back at some of the dark times my vision suddenly becomes 20/20 and yours can as well.

Believe me, God is good. But His goodness shows in his time and not our time. He has moved mountains and He can help you overcome your adversities. It may take time, but there is a plan for each of us. We simply need to take the time to discover it and allow the plan to be carried out. I believe the hand of God will be evident in each of the following situations. Slip ups and trip ups? Rather adversities I survived that made me remember to never forget where I came from.

I went through school without motivation and most likely with an undiagnosed attention deficit disorder. I am not blaming anyone. These kinds of diagnoses were unheard of during my elementary years. Things were different back then. Academically I was "not college material" and was reminded of this at every possible occasion. I had my life totally planned on falsehoods. What did I have to worry about? I could have worked for my dad in the paper industry after high school. It was a very good profession in those days. Many of my family, friends and acquaintances worked in the paper industry during the '60s and '70s.

I had no intention of continuing with school and only began the practical nursing program at the local vocational school because I needed the 2.5 credits to graduate. Then I made the decision (with much encouragement) to continue the nursing program believing I would be an LPN for my career. Those three letters following my name were important. At least to me. I wasn't college material, so this was the best I was going to do. I had no idea that many years later I would complete a doctoral degree. Who would have thought? I can assure you God did! It certainly was a surprise to me until I walked onto the stage at my Doctoral Commencement Ceremony.

If I was in charge, would I have allowed myself to be unsuccessful in any exam? I think not. Fortunately, I was chosen by wonderful parents, and I successfully completed the exam and my degree. I'm aware it is easily said but not so easily done. When we are stuck in these dark places and the weight of the world seems to be on us, it's not easy to pay yourself some positivity.

Up my sleeve I've got one of my major slip-ups. It is an adversity from way back in high school. You may as well call it one of the most prized members of my adversity bank. It brings backs laughter as well as the thought that sometimes we have invisible walls of protection around us. It also brings back one of the loudest "oh, shit" moments ever.

My sister purchased her first car when I was in high school. It was a Mustang. I'm not sure what year, but it may have been a 1962. Being two years younger than her, I didn't have a license or permit to drive. Nonetheless, my sister, as awesome as always, gave me my own set of keys to that beast on wheels. I could "sit in it" and "listen to the radio", while she attended vocational school in the next town. There was a delay between high school students going home and students returning from vocational programs, so I would sit in her car and wait for a ride home. How bad could that be? After all, I couldn't drive.

The vocational students went home on a later bus, but I had the keys to this shiny medium to dark blue mustang, crowned by a classy white top. So there I would be, for the hour or so it took for her to return and drive us home.

Day after day and week after week I practiced this ritual. Word got out that I had the keys to her car. Soon a classmate asked if he could join me for a ride home. Of course, I agreed. We completed the same ritual for another few weeks until we came up with a mutual agreement (I am not certain who had the idea, and it doesn't matter) to take the car for short rides. How bad would it be?

First, we drove around the school parking lot, after the buses had gone. The parking lot was nearly empty after high school was dismissed because all the students who had cars had driven off.

This short drive continued for days and then we started traveling the local back roads. The rides were pleasant and we had it under control. Then my classmate asked if he could drive. Why not? I don't believe I said yes at first, but things gradually took that turn, leaving us taking turns driving up and down this one straightaway to see who could go faster.

Back and forth we went several times before returning to the school parking lot without incident. We were both fifteen and full of mischief. Shhh.... don't tell. No harm done yet.

One beautiful sunny autumn day we took our usual ride after school. Except this time, we ventured away from the straightaway onto other roads. We never adjusted the speed. On this bright and sunny fall day I drove into a driveway, cut across the lawn of that house, circled back to the highway and stepped on the gas.

As we rounded a nearly ninety-degree curve, I lost control of the car, and we spun around, and guess what? We kept spinning. The sound system's speakers flew out of the open windows and the car sailed into a ditch. Coming to rest inches from the side of a barn, I knew in that moment it was truly the heaviest "oh shit" moment I ever had. The ditch wasn't too deep, and I was able to drive the car back onto the road.

There was some damage, but fear took over and I headed back to the school parking lot to park right in the space where we had started out. What I didn't count on was the tires going flat. Every one of the tires was nothing but rubber. Not an ounce of air. I drove what sounded like a logging truck or a derailed train coming down the road.

By the time we returned to school, all four rims were flattened out and we were traveling on flattened metal. Metal to pavement. Just imagine the sound and the feeling you got driving the car like that.

I should have gotten some type of credit for handling a vehicle in that shape. Voila! Awaiting our arrival was one patrol car from the county sheriff's office. After our quiet return the second patrol car arrived. Following some preliminary questioning, my parents arrived, and so did my sister and a bus load of vocational students. Our adventure was now part of local small-town gossip.

The rest of the story isn't what makes my point. The point lies in what you have read so far. I've listened to pastors on occasion; they describe our "wall of protection." My classmate and I certainly had one in this situation. Mom and dad were not very happy, but they were both glad to see us alive after hearing the story. The Miranda Warning was read to me. I have a copy of the statement somewhere around the house today, certain it was never thrown away.

My Miranda Warning was given after mom had a long discussion with the deputy. I was only fifteen. Not at the time, but today I believe they were working together on what to do with us. My sister could not press charges because she didn't want to do that to her little brother and after all she had provided the keys. My classmate and I were forbidden from seeing each other and I was informed that instead of being allowed to get a driver's permit that August, I would have to wait for the following year (nearly 2 years).

I suspect the deputy was satisfied with the outcome. Oh, and I also had to pay to have my sister's car repaired. Fortunately, she was dating a "body mechanic" at the time, but three hundred dollars then for a fifteen-year-old seemed like thousands. We also had to clean up the ruts we left in one of the farmhouse yards.

"I've learned more from my mistakes than I ever have from doing something right."

Mark209

The car was repaired, life went on, my classmate and I occasionally talk about this today and I believe we continue to have that "wall of protection." During this time, I know it wasn't my faith, but the faith of my mom that undoubtedly provided the wall. Sometimes you've got to have faith that someone else is praying for you.

But let all who take refuge and put their trust in You rejoice, let them ever sing for joy; Because You cover and shelter them, let those who love Your name be joyful and exult in You.

Psalm 5:11 (AMP)

We are going to have the "Oh shit" moments. No one promised us a perfect and smooth journey. It is many years later and I tell you friends, Satan perches on our shoulders, but if we have faith and God in our hearts, we can knock him off. My faith has been tested over and over and it was generally my own fault.

Being negative can destroy you and make it difficult for you to continue to move forward. Staying positive through faith can catapult

115

you forward. Fortunately for me, many of my "God doesn't exist" episodes happened in my younger years. As time passes, I still make mistakes, but I continue making strides to develop my relationship with my God. Satan sits talking in one ear, while God shouts inside my head. Sometimes I just need to stop and listen and so do you.

He protected us on our entire journey and among all the nations through which we traveled.

Joshua 24: 17 (NIV)

IX

The Right Way

"Because he has his heart set on me, I will deliver him; I will protect him because he knows my name. When he calls out to me, I will answer him; I will be with him in trouble. I will rescue him and give him honor."

Psalm 91:14-15

A million times have we heard that there is only one *right way*. Right way? Can there be only one right way? Who am I to tell you the "right way" for doing anything anyway? I learned more from the wrong way(s). I hope you find the "right way" for yourself through what I share. And if not the right way, then the best way for you. But I insist that it's essential to have faith in yourself and have trust and advocacy during your journey. There are always two sides, and you need to find the truth from there on.

117

After receiving a bad grade in an elementary school geography test, my mother reviewed the test. I'd been unsuccessful. Upon mom's testing me, I verbally answered the questions, but the error lay in my spelling the answers. It was obvious I had learned the geography information. Mom advocated for me with my teacher who agreed that I knew the geography information but was unable to spell (thankfully we have a spell checker today). The teacher asked mom if she thought spelling correctly was important and she agreed. However, the test was on geography and not spelling. I believe mom defended her position and mine well and I passed the test. Spelling would continue to be a struggle for me, but we worked on it throughout the rest of my time in fourth grade. And I continue to work on spelling today. But I've got this.

As children our most trusted and precious advocate(s) are primarily our parent(s). They will be our advocates in any situation (even if we are wrong). We can trust them with our lives and without a doubt at times our lives are totally entrusted to them.

Trust is difficult to find at times. Who can you trust especially in a world that is such a mess? Who can be trusted? Perhaps you're at a point in your life where you need someone to confide in. A person who will have your back through the dark times could be your advocate. Why's having an advocate important? A true advocate is a person who supports you publicly and you can be sure has your best interest at heart. Life brings many opportunities that require us to have advocacy. At the same time, it also gives us chances to advocate for others.

Everyone should look out not only for his own interests, but for the interests of others.

Philippians 2:4

According to Merriam-Webster, trust is a firm belief in the character, strength, or truth of someone or something; a person or thing in which confidence is placed. It is essential to have confidence in someone or several individuals, but you must trust yourself. The trust you place in yourself that you can make the correct decision; the confidence that you can achieve your dreams lets Lady Success know you're one to look out for.

They will have no fear of bad news; Their hearts are steadfast, trusting in the Lord.

Psalm 112:7 (NIV)

Walking out from under our parents' wings, later in life, your closest friend, husband, wife,

119

partner can play the role of advocate. If they will stand beside you in all situations, you can be assured you have the trust essential to a relationship. Knowing you have got someone as your advocate is a blessing.

But I will send you the Advocate – the Spirit of truth.

John 15:26

When your advocate is your soul mate, then it may not be necessary to say a word before you're understood. If you haven't discovered this person yet, keep searching. If you are a college student, please find an academic advisor who is your advocate. You should be supported throughout your academic journey. Don't allow anyone to cut your legs out from under you. If you are making an honest attempt, the faculty should be doing the same to support you and encouraging your success.

Even now my witness is in heaven; my advocate is on high.

Job 16:19 (NIV)

My Christian belief instills into me that I should be confident of having my God as my ultimate advocate. I have called on Him in many situations and that is what brought me this far in life.

"Now faith is the reality of what is hoped for, the proof of what is not seen."

Hebrews 11:1

I also know my witnesses are in heaven; my advocates remain mom, dad and I know my grandmother. When I wasn't praying, they were. I know mom was. Someone was. While writing this chapter I came across a written passage in my daily devotional, by Diane Neal Matthews. It ended like this:

"How comforting to know that Jesus is serving as my advocate in heaven. He comes against anything and anyone who tries to condemn me. He stands ready to mediate on my behalf in every detail of my life. Knowing that the one who loves me most intercedes for me in heaven gives me courage to face anything that happens on the earth."

Thank you, Dianne, for these truths. I know I have an advocate. Do you?

"Ask, and it will be given to you. Seek, and you will find. Knock, and the door will be opened to you."

Matthew 7:7

If doubts regarding your academic journey stump you, you must find an academic

121

advocate. Find a faculty member who will help you respond to the issues, and encourage you with sound guidance. Find the advocate who has "never forgotten where they came from." An advisor who is grounded in faith and does not counsel from a position of negativism would bring your hidden strengths to the fore. The last thing you need is another dark person to amplify your dark times. You should look for a mentor or advisor who leads with positive thinking. Instead of the "why you can't" you need to request someone to help you out with the "this is how you can."

"Positive thinking will let you do everything better than negative thinking will."

Zig Ziglar

In case your academic institution does not have this kind of advocate, I recommend you search for a vocational program that will provide the support you need for your dreams. Avoid shaded and false guidance at all costs. Beware of faculty who provide advocacy on a quid pro quo basis. Read the mission of the school, college or university and do a serious background investigation. Find current students. Ask if they have an academic advocate. You are going to experience some low places throughout your academic journey, and the last thing you need is faculty with negative thinking. Beware of faculty with biases. They are the most dangerous.

It pays to take life seriously; things work out when you trust in God.

Proverbs 16:20 (MSG)

Passing everyone or providing remedial assignments to improve your grade is not advocacy and at some point (perhaps on the NCLEX for nurses, LSATs for law school, MCATs for medical school) it will catch up with you. It might happen when you think it's least possible. You are not going to get extra credit work in life.

Believe me, there are faculty in every school, college or university who will recognize your potential, understand your difficult times, and support you when necessary. Find the academic institution and faculty who are forthright, honest, and who can remember and understand where they came from.

The struggling student is always close to my heart. I've never forgotten where I came from. I have supported individuals who simply needed a shoulder to rest their head on, besides putting every effort into a student who was making a second attempt.

I am sure of this, that he who started a good work in you will carry it on to completion.

Philippians 1:6

In life do the same. Find the advocate who will never let you down and who is there to help pick you up when you fall. Search for those individuals who are honest, trustworthy, supportive, and who work to lift others up and not put them down. Remember, it remains important to have faith in others, faith in your own self, and faith in God.

And I will ask the father, and he will give you another Advocate, who will never leave you.

John 14:16

Not everyone who starts school, nursing school, college, or university successfully completes their program. Yet the road you take leads you somewhere. Perhaps it will take more than one attempt to reach your desired destination. Remember, I entered nursing school for 2.5 credits so I could graduate high school in three years instead of four.

Blessed is the man who believes and trusts in and relies on the Lord

Jeremiah 17:7 (AMP)

Over forty years later the road has taken me places I could never have imagined.

Each one of us is to please his neighbor for his good, to build him up.

Romans 15:1

Your journey may begin in a nursing program, but you may find your way into a totally different career. You may begin in an MBA program, and you may become a teacher, or you might start on the way to priesthood and become a nurse. What is important is that you begin the journey believing in yourself and you complete the journey discovering your purpose.

"Biblical hope is the greatest source of optimism in the world. It's relentless, rewarding, and the essence of personal revival."

David Jeremiah

Always keep in mind that God knew you and planned your life. He designed a purpose that is stored up for you and it will last your lifetime. Remember it is not on our time schedule, but the one that has been set for us.

"The future is as bright as the promises of God."
William Carey

A friend encouraged me to apply for a nursing position at the local prison after I had completed my associate degree. First question that passed my lips was, "What does a nurse do in prison?" I was in my mid-twenties and after discovering many prisons have hospitals and clinic areas, I applied and I was hired. I went to work as an RN in a maximum-security prison. What the hell was I thinking? A few years later I didn't doubt that this was certainly not going to be the career I had in mind.

The games staff played were just as vicious as those the inmates played at times. I respectfully resigned and went on to experience other areas of nursing practice. Nearly ten years later I would return to correctional nursing, where it would become an amazing career with so many wonderful opportunities. It was exactly where I needed to be to get a wonderful career going. As you will see later, my return to correctional nursing was preceded by a dark time. The return was the light that provided many blessings. It carved out an outstanding career and a personal purpose.

The fear of man brings a snare. But whoever trusts in and puts his confidence in the Lord will be exalted and safe.

Proverbs 29:25 (AMP)

Each of us will go through a dark time when it may seem that our faith has gone on vacation. You're going to be sure that you've been forgotten. In these times, when we close the doors to God, we deprive ourselves of a master plan. That plan can spell wonders for us at a psychological as well as sociological level. Believing only helps us seek further. It's not an end in itself. Someone somewhere is waiting to hand you the key to the box which hides your purpose.

So, confide in Him and allow Him to provide direction. God has a great deal in store for each of us. We need the patience to seek his strength in our time of need.

Once again, as I get older, I need His strength more. I recommend this approach for you. After all it can't hurt.

Now may the God who gives endurance and who supplies encouragement grant that you be of the same mind with one another according to Christ Jesus,

Romans 15:5 (AMP)

The "right way" for me was to develop my relationship with God. It led me up a path to success the "right way." Although difficult to follow, it's well worth the journey. It's only a question of how long it takes you to find the advocate who helps you discover that "right way" for you.

"I am sure of this, that he who started a good work in you will carry it on to completion."

Philippians 1:6

Could Not Imagine

Priority in caring for others has forever been at the forefront of my life. I am so fortunate that this is a priority for my life partner as well. Chosen and raised by parents who always put others first, I watched my mom care for my grandparents — as did my wife and I. Many families could not be further apart when it comes to caring for others. Especially in providing care for our aging loved ones or keeping an eye on an elderly neighbor. Are we living in different worlds?

I have lifetime friends who provided care for their parent(s) until the time of their passing. Families came together under the roof as provisions were made to provide care at home. Not everyone is lucky to be raised in such a home. Some individuals believe the aging, elderly parent is simply a burden. They are viewed as worn out, used up, and so they can be discarded. Our senior citizens have much to offer us through wisdom and knowledge and yet they age alone. Like hunger, unemployment and poverty; this too deserves to be counted as a deep social deprivation of our times.

I suspect coming from being unwanted at birth may have something to do with how I believe we should care for our parent(s) as they age. Of course, I could never give back what my parents gave me.

Even though I don't want to judge, I will acknowledge that if you were raised in an abusive or unsecure home, there may be cause for walking away; and perhaps it is understandable. I'm not certain what causes some to turn from their folks, after receiving a loving home with parents who provided the best they could. I have noted daughters seem to have a connection with their fathers and similarly sons have a connection with their mothers. It's plain to see something binds them. If you missed this experience, my heart truly breaks for you.

The elderly population was more vulnerable during the world COVID crisis. We came up with the idea of giving construction paper to those residing in the senior complex near our home. With sheets of red, yellow, and green construction paper, they could place chosen colors in the window so we should receive a signal. Green meant everything was good; yellow if they needed something but not immediately; and red said they needed assistance in a hurry. Throughout the pandemic we watched their windows several times a day. Whenever a yellow or a red came up, we knew what to do. It was a small part of caring and they all appreciated it so much. How much more should we give our own?

I live with one major regret — an adversity I continue to deal with; not having the chance of a conversation with my mother alone in the days prior to her passing. Might I have insisted her to seek intervention for her medical condition? Did I have a period of turning away from my mother? Will this adversity make me stronger? Will I overcome it? Is it my atonement to live the remainder of my life secretly haunted by this thought?

The *should-have's* and *could-have's* won't change the outcome. Here is where my faith must take over. Don't put yourself in this place. Believe me it is the darkest place I ever spent time in.

Listen to your father who gave you life, and do not despise your mother when she is old.

Proverbs 23:22

Questions wrestle inside my head when I turn back to thoughts about my mother's last days. It is much like having a room in the house you seldom step into, because the lights always flicker out every time you do. Sometimes I believe it will remain dark in there until my final day.

Why did mom stop taking her medication? Did she believe she was burdening me? Or was there another impulse behind cutting off the life-sustaining intervention?

I will always have questions regarding her last days and hours. The one which gnaws at me most is: Did I let her go, without asking the right questions?

Sometimes knowing too much will not help you the least. The questions are like voices trapped inside that dark room. If I start exploring all of them, this chapter will brim with what I didn't do. I don't mean it to be about that. I want it to be about the things we did and what we should do for our aging parents.

132

Someone wrote to me once, stating, "I don't want to be a burden for my children. My kids have busy lives and have their own kids to take care of. They don't need another 'kid'. I just hope I live long and healthy enough that they don't have to!"

I contend: Didn't you have a busy life while raising them?

I realize some children don't have the ability or means to have a parent live in the same home or nearby. And now I can even understand because another cycle is nearing its end as the child of yesterday now sits — an aging parent — at his desk writing this chapter.

It's not easy looking out at a house which now only echoes with the life, love and laughter that once grew within its walls all day long. I've put a timer on the lights, so the house isn't dark in the evening anymore. Yet, I can't close my eyes to the fact that it's going to be empty a great deal of the time.

Sometimes a parent or an older individual will not ask for assistance because they don't want to come across as a hindrance. Yet, it's not a big deal to take timeout to visit for an hour. In doing so, one could easily pick up a few items at the store or the pharmacy on the way down to their place. Whether it's a parent or an elderly neighbor, it's simply a matter of calling ahead to ask what they may need — especially if you know you're going to pass that way. But we need to take a moment to think of someone other than ourselves, to want to act on such small impulses of kindness.

It's simply a 'me' and 'my' attitude when we don't make the first call. In a world that's increasingly turning to be all about the 'me', it's not intuitive in the least to forget people around us in their advanced age may need a helping hand.

Was it all about 'me' when mom probably needed me most? You feel nothing before but once the regret holes up in your heart, believe me, nothing could make you feel worse. I wish you never feel a similar regret.

It's natural to feel our aging parent has become a nuisance. We made our parents feel the same at times when we were little but that didn't make them turn their backs on us for good. Didn't you ever feel your elderly parent was anything but a blessing? You know what I'm talking about. We become complacent to the sacrifices they made for us. Instead of taking them into our home where they are safe, we tend to put them in nursing homes.

We would rather have someone else fulfill the responsibility for their care. Why should I lose my precious time when someone else in the family can be made in-charge? In seeing the aged members of our community as outdated relics, we impoverish ourselves of their wisdom.

Support widows who are genuinely in need. But if any widow has children or grandchildren, let them learn to practice godliness toward their own family first and to repay their parents, for this pleases God.

1 Timothy 5:3-4

On the other hand, there are parents in their advanced stage, who dislike constant supervision. They would rather surround themselves by individuals their own age than stay at their child's home. Nevertheless, the obligation to our parents is biblical.

Should they need financial assistance, we must help. When they become ill, we should provide care. If they need a place to stay, our homes should be open. If they need assistance with their independence, we should help them maintain it. We should be stepping up to make sure the parent has love and care. What better love could there be for a parent than the love of their child? Empathy is a rare commodity these days. Remember how they cared when we were vulnerable, and it might be worlds easier to return the gesture. The cares of the world are not large enough to make us forget where we're coming from, are they?

Honor your father and mother – which is the first commandment with a promise "that it may go well with you and that you may enjoy long life on the earth"

Ephesians 6:2-3

I'd forgotten for a moment where I came from. It changed me for the rest of my life. Don't let the dark place invite you. The *You're a good son* has less meaning when you let the 'you' come before 'them'. Lest it turn into an adversity you might never overcome.

XI

Something Wasn't Right

Have you ever felt the pit of your stomach churn with that feeling? The moment when a little voice squirms its way out of your subconscious, telling you something is about to happen? It is perhaps one of the mysteries of human perception, but you can see it coming when it does. You cannot shake off the feeling that something isn't right.

In this chapter I want to share with you some of my something-wasn't-right experiences. Reflecting on them today I realize they were some of my best "opportunity" moments. A suspicion that something was heading my way gripped me, and no matter what I did, I couldn't counter the feeling that it would be unpleasant. But nothing could have surprised me more than the outcome when I discovered the foreboding led me to success.

137

So, let me begin by sharing the incident from my childhood that brought on this experience. Although at the time, the feeling didn't hit me directly, but my parents couldn't deny it. Had it not been for divine intervention, likely my sister and I may not be here today. Fortunately for us, our parents felt the strong surge that, "something wasn't right."

We began family camping with friends when we were in elementary school. From cabin camping, we progressed to tent camping, then "pop-up" camping, and finally a travel trailer. If we found out that friends were camping nearby, we would head over because mom and dad didn't want to miss a game of cards. Many of their friends enjoyed a good game of pinochle and they would play for hours.

On this one occasion mom and dad played late into the night while my sister and I slept on one of the beds in the pop-up camper. To ward off the chill of the night, a kerosene heater had been placed in the center of the camper. Perhaps many of you can already see where this story is headed.

When the game was finally finished, my sister and I were gathered up for the trip home. I cannot recall all the specifics of the incident, but I have relied on mom's recollection over the years. She says we had been sleeping in the camper for hours with the kerosene heater running. Dad moved us to the car, which he had left idling. Mom noticed we were like "wet dish rags." She always came up with unique terms of describing us when we were sick.

We were not as fully awake as mom would have expected. My sister seemed a bit confused by the movement. That's not unusual for a small girl of fifty to sixty pounds, is it?

Apparently, both of us were having difficulty waking up. We were loaded into the backseat of the car for the journey back home. Seatbelts were not required at the time. The heat was on stun and the car was more than warm. As I understand, we both began to vomit. Mom believed the car was too hot, so dad turned the heat down and opened his window. Although we were waking up a bit more by now, nausea hit us like a rock in the face. We vomited during the entire trip home.

I am sure it wasn't a pleasant trip for mom and dad. Mom tended to worry a great deal as I have already mentioned. I am certain her anxiety was hitting the roof during this situation. She had known something just wasn't right.

Was it divine intervention? Most assuredly it was. That's why the symptoms did not play out too much to our disadvantage. Weakness, dizziness, nausea, vomiting, disorientation, loss of consciousness – all these point to carbon monoxide poisoning. Had someone (and I will call this someone God) not directed the card game to end at the exact time it did, how much more would my sister and I have breathed in, before a permanent damage or death? I will believe it was God who interceded.

Carbon monoxide can play havoc on individuals who are sleeping or even intoxicated. It can lead to irreversible brain damage, or one may even die before anyone realizes it. Our parents had no idea while they played cards and reflecting on the situation, it is evident we were unintentionally poisoned by the heater. So, was it divine intervention? Absolutely! There must have been a purpose for us.

In the same way the Spirit helps us in our weakness. We do not know what prayer to offer or how to offer it as we should, but the Spirit Himself (knows our need and at the right time) intercedes on our behalf with sighs and groanings too deep for words.

Romans 8:26 (AMP)

My intercessor is my friend as my eyes pour out tears to God

Job 16:20 (NIV)

*For since the creation of the world God's invisible qualities, his eternal power and **divine** nature have been clearly seen, being understood from what has been made, so that people are without excuse.*

Romans 1:20 (NIV)

There is no doubt we are alive today by the grace of God. The possible outcomes from that situation are enough to make me shudder. Adversity to success! We live on with no permanent damage.

And the child grew and became strong; he was filled with wisdom, and the grace of God was on him.

Luke 2:40 (NIV)

I mentioned that one of the stops on the winding course of my career was a job in a maximum-security prison. Back then, in my mid-twenties, I realized something wasn't right. It was a feeling without a shape or name, but it didn't stop me going to work. I had been married several years. I don't imagine I was anywhere ready to work in that setting. My family was young and, in many respects, so was I.

Yes, I had the education and the license, but I lacked a maturity essential to work in that kind of vulnerable setting. Young men and women, who are still wet behind the ears enter employment in a correctional facility, but it's worth asking if they are mentally braced to handle the exposure; especially so, when the challenges of the environment might lead to an over-exposure.

I have seen families torn apart by alcohol, drugs, and some ended in divorce, because of encountering this stressful environment daily for several years. Thus, I knew then, that something wasn't right.

One evening after work I threatened to *keep-lock* one of our sons. That is when I knew something had to change. Keep-lock is a term used in prisons when the inmate is secured in a cell for 23 out of 24 hours a day as a disciplinary measure. You just don't "keep-lock" your children. I was bringing the stressors of work home. Shortly following this incident, I noticed my tolerance fuse getting shorter, the longer I stayed in that environment.

I resigned and began a position as a unit coordinator in a long-term care facility where I opened a traumatic brain injury unit. At the same time, I was also working during the summer, at a local scout camp. I had the most awesome and amazing experiences at camp during the summer and developed friendships that would continue for many years. Some continue even today.

About 2-3 miles from the summer camp where we worked the building adventure of our lives was taking place in the country. As the dream home progressed, we knew 'something wasn't right.' It was a big mistake to be our own general contractor.

We still hadn't been able to move into the house by mid-October and the camp for Scouts had already closed. The kitchen was not finished, and we had no appliances. They will not issue a certificate of occupancy without a kitchen.

The camp director/ranger informed us that the water in the camp had to be shut off soon. He and another friend from camp offered to help us finish the house, so we could move in.

We had already paid for the house to be completed.

We spoke with a specific building contractor, who was to deliver a ten-thousand-dollar kitchen (that was an expensive kitchen at the time). What we received were three-hundred-dollar unfinished pine cabinets and no appliances. We purchased a stove and used several coolers until we could get a refrigerator, and we moved in. The house was built with electric heat and had a cathedral ceiling.

We were cold most of the time and to keep the house warm the electric bill was larger than our mortgage. So, we had a very nice wood-burning stove installed. It helped with the heat but chopping and stacking wood wasn't something we wanted to do into our elder years.

Our youngest would be born while we were living in the log home. By the time he was ready for kindergarten we had sold our dream home and purchased a house that was nearly two-hundred-year-old in the nearby village. Same town and school district as our dream log home. We reside in that home today and it has become our dream home.

Though the Lord gives you the bread of adversity and the water of oppression, yet your teacher will no longer hide Himself, but your eyes see your teacher.

Isaiah 30:20 (AMP)

When the camp director/ranger announced, he was going to retire, the local Boy Scout council called to fill up two positions: District Executive and Ranger.

I wanted to be camp director, but I doubted if I had what it took to replace the previous camp ranger at the camp where we had been working during the summers. Serving as director was one thing, but a ranger I was not. Handyman skills were not my calling. Funny thing, my dad had built our family home and a beautiful home it was. It is inhabited by a family to this day.

Sadly, I've never been able to cut a straight line. I knew if I became a district executive for the local council, there was a very good chance I could be camp director, given my scouting and summer camp experience.

Side Note:

While writing this section I received a text and picture from one of the camp staff families that

I have been describing, and who we have known for over thirty years. The text read:

"Almost heaven West Virginia..." and above it is a picture of three staff members, including myself, playing guitar. I would imagine we were singing Country Roads. Is this coincidence or the guiding hands of God?

Sadly, not long after a wonderful camp staff reunion, this beloved staff member, who is in the photo playing guitars with me, passed away. I am thankful for the text message.

I inquired about the district executive position and completed the process required to become a professional scouter. Apparently, the individual administering the verbal portion of the screening believed I somehow knew how to respond to the questions. I answered them as I believed the scouting program was designed, and I guess I was spot on. I scored very high on this part of the screening.

This would also be the spring and summer when both of my grandparents would pass away. My grandfather passed away seventy-two days after my grandmother. We had been their primary care providers for several years. It was time to leave nursing.

A few months later I was offered and accepted a district executive position and was asked to direct the summer camping program. I did so, for five seasons. On a professional level, those five years were mostly an enjoyable experience. The best part of the position was serving as the summer camp director. I was ready to accept a promotion to Senior District Executive and was offered an interview in Dalton, MA. We packed up and headed east, finally arrived, and following the interview I was immediately offered the position of district executive. Something "just wasn't right." As we listened, it was obvious I was being offered a district executive position (no promotion) and they would *try me out*. If I turned out successful, they would offer me a senior position.

We returned home, I returned to the office, and the scout executive wanted the story. I informed him that I had turned down the offer as it was not a promotion. I also expressed my displeasure in being misled to travel several hours only to sit in an interview for a position I was already serving. He just sat with a blank look on his face and then offered to make a phone call. I approved. Following the call, I would later simply refuse the position. Something just "wasn't right."

On a personal level, it would be during this same period that my wife would become ill following the birth of our youngest son. None of the family neither close friends had any idea what was happening. The council scout executive took a very heartless approach. It was during this period that I saw, "something wasn't right."

The camping season passed, and I was away to care for my family. While I was trying to make sure what was happening with my wife, I got a call from the scout executive saying someone else would be acting as camp director. He advised it would do the council good since the attention of the district executives would be on "fundraising." I was not, nor will I ever be, a professional fundraiser.

A few weeks passed and some of the council's camping-committee members, executive board members, and the scout executive called a meeting. I took the opportunity to announce I had come to a decision. Everyone around the table looked on with anticipation, thinking I had reconsidered the promotion and was going to tell them I was moving to Dalton, MA. I announced that I would be leaving the scouts and return to the nursing profession.

I said I was going to be a health coordinator/educator, in two weeks, for a private organization caring for individuals with developmental disabilities. After enjoying the initial shock on their faces, I left the office. I knew, "something wasn't right."

Two weeks passed and I began my health coordinator/educator career. I enjoyed teaching and I had had prior experience with the vulnerable population, whose health care I was going to manage. It was wonderful and I had an amazing supervisor. Funny thing is my supervisor was an LPN and I was an RN at the time. I don't think that is possible, but I was new. It wasn't long and the LPN asked if I would serve as the nursing director. The necessary approvals were obtained, and I was promoted to the director of nursing for the agency.

My responsibilities changed a bit but I continued to provide health coordinator services and instruction for the employees of the agency. It was a place where the clients received the best services. Then one day, "something wasn't right."

I was asked to meet with the agency director at noon. Apparently, you didn't want a noon meeting with this person. I had had several

149

prior meetings, and we had enjoyed some great laughs together. But on this day, I was informed I no longer had a position effective 1:00 p.m. I just sat there. I believe my mouth just hung open. I had several years of exemplary evaluations and promotions. Something wasn't right.

It was later brought to my attention, this executive director felt threatened by any male administrator who did outstanding work. Guess she thought someone could replace her. Actually, none of us wanted her job. Following my elimination, each male was systematically eliminated from administrative positions in the agency. Something wasn't right.

I was provided a severance package and benefits that would last an adequate amount of time for me to find gainful employment. I was devastated. I had a young family and all the responsibilities that go with that position. What was I going to do?

Several of us who were systematically removed sought legal action, but nothing ever became of the case. Inside some box, in an attorney's office, sits several years of outstanding documentation. Case closed. Moving on.

This dark place made me grow. I suspect now I would have to thank her for her heartlessness. You see, the adversity eventually became a success. It led me to a wonderful career in State service. With the best salary and benefits, my family would be well-cared for.

Be wise in the way you act toward outsiders; make the most of every opportunity.

Colossians 4:5 (NIV)

Be very careful, then, how you live – not as unwise but as wise, making the most of every opportunity, because the days are evil. Therefore, do not be foolish, but understand what the Lord's will is.

Ephesians 5:15-17 (NIV)

When a door is closed, a window is opened. In many instances, the maxim is real. You have got to judge when an opportunity is within your reach. Within a couple of weeks, I had been hired for a position in correctional health care at a local medium-security facility. This would change the trajectory of my life for the rest of my career. It helped me discover my calling. Did you hear me say a career in correctional health care? Ten years prior, this wasn't a career for me. All things are in God's time and can certainly surprise us. I truly don't recall any "something wasn't right" moments during the twenty-five years devoted to the health care of this vulnerable population.

During this period, I promoted several times. The roles I used to imagine serving in, wanted my professional attention, turning my expectations into reality. Finding a success story in the corridors of a correctional health institute is hard to believe.

This professional position gave way to resuming school. Not only did I complete a Bachelor of Science in Nursing but finished graduate school and moved on to complete a doctorate degree.

Thank you for eliminating my position so many years ago. If not for that, I'd never have made it out of the drably predictable, to benefit from some of the most amazing professionals. It's almost a pity how some people will never break through their insecurity to taste true professional development. I retired with ease and continue to consult and instruct in correctional health care.

Deceit is in the hearts of those who plot evil, but those who promote peace have joy.

152

Proverbs 12:20 (NIV)

Something wasn't right, was it?

Sometime in the late 1990s, I developed an interest in returning to school. It wasn't so much about furthering my degree in nursing than the realization that I needed to advance my education for promotional opportunities.

I sought out and found a program in Health Care Administration. Along with my degree of associate in nursing, this education may be beneficial. So, I enrolled at a university I believed provided an accredited education. I was verbally informed when I called them that they were absolutely accredited. They provided accreditation documentation for their program.

After paying several thousands of dollars, working through all the necessary assignments for an advanced degree, receiving information about commencement regalia; even being informed what colors would be inside the regalia hood, as well as other graduation requirements. Surprise! There was no university. Receiving a university degree and finding out it's a worthless piece of paper, doesn't provide a positive perspective.

I discovered it was a diploma mill that had formerly operated out of Louisiana under a different name. These fraudsters had operated out of Hawaii and Mississippi under yet another name. My 2002 diploma was as valuable as tissue paper. I was devastated.

In 2004, a school district in Michigan commenced legal action against two of their faculty who planned on enrolling in a doctoral course through this same university to increase their salaries. This action ultimately resulted in further investigation, leading to revelations about Cambridge State University being a diploma mill with an extensive criminal history.

For me this was too little too late. It was like I had burned thousands of dollars in a campfire. I had the ultimate punch in the gut.

And then in 2009, I grabbed myself by the bootstraps and made the decision to never be taken in again. I was going to complete an advanced degree come hell or high water. Even, if it took until my retirement. This time securing all proof that the university I attended was indeed a regionally accredited university.

I moved forward with a Bachelor of Science in Nursing and was promoted with the department of corrections. My supervisor wanted everyone on her team to have a master's degree, so I completed that.

I suspect my prior, not so wonderful academic experience, lit a fire under my backside. In 2016, I graduated with distinction with a Doctor of Nursing Practice. And yes, from a fully accredited university. The rest is history. I never forgot where I came from.

Adversity to success! Not a path I recommend, but a success, nonetheless.

As luck would have it, I received a call from the clinical placement staff at a local private college during the winter of 2014-2015. Out of the blue, they wanted to know if I was interested in a weekend clinical adjunct position. Remember I had always wanted to be a teacher? I went for the meeting and in January of 2015 began my academic journey as a clinical adjunct.

What was more? I could keep my position in correctional health care. Serving as a weekend clinical instructor during the spring semester of 2015, I got a call one day asking if there was a chance of me wanting to opt for a position with the practical nursing program. This program was held on weekends and once again fit in well with my full-time employment.

So, in the fall of 2015, as part of the program, I lectured in mental health and leadership.

I cherished the experience, and in the spring of 2016, I celebrated commencement with my first graduating class. The thoughtful gift they presented me hangs in my office today. They knew I have a love for eagles, so they had a print of an eagle's head made, matted, and framed. Everyone signed it, and they presented it to me at the "White Tea."

Dr. Blair, thank you for everything! You were the calming force we all needed thank you for making our dreams a reality.

K. N. LPN

Class of 2016

Dr. Blair, although we were all apprehensive about having a new teacher this semester, we couldn't have asked for a better mentor, or cheerleader to help shape us and help us to be the best we could be! Thank you so much for everything you did for us! I will be forever grateful!

Dr. Blair, thank you for everything! You helped shape us into the RNs we are now! You are amazing!

C. S. LPN

Class of 2016

RN Class of 2018

Dr. Blair, thank you for being behind us from day one. You are an incredible teacher. It has been a true pleasure...

Thank you, Doc, for all the years of guidance and encouragement...

R. B. LPN

Class of 2016

RN Class of 2018

"White Tea" is very specific to this nursing program. For most nursing programs it is traditionally known as a "pinning ceremony." The White Tea was typically held around afternoon tea, but tea is not served. Nursing students wear white and are presented with their nursing school pins. It is a very moving ceremony. All nurses and student nurses recite the Nightingale Pledge with glowing candles following their pinning.

This would have been a "capping ceremony" in years past when each nursing program had their individual caps representing the school. It is a very beautiful ceremony. The student officially passes from being a student nurse into the nursing profession.

In the spring of 2016, I would complete my doctorate in nursing practice. Spring 2016 also brought an offer to serve as full-time faculty at the college. Given some thought and review of how it would impact my retirement from the state, I accepted. In June of 2016 I retired from state employment and began my full-time journey in academia. My role was clinical instructor in mental health during the fall semester and instructor in mental health content. In the spring I covered some medical surgical nursing topics and was a clinical instructor on a vascular unit. I was enjoying the experience and knew this is where God had placed me. The department chair asked repeatedly if I had any regrets. Absolutely not! This would later change when something wasn't right. A friend (my car driving partner in high school) noted on Facebook how wonderful it was, at the end of my career I would do what I wanted to do as a kid, and he was right.

The years passed and I was promoted from instructor to assistant professor. The evaluations from students were encouraging and the one written assessment I received during my tenure made some great points but was also good. I began writing items (questions) for the National Council School Boards of Nursing (NCSBN) PN and RN exams. It was a great learning and networking experience. As time passed, I enjoyed many wonderful days and evenings with faculty, staff, and students. A unique opportunity was created. My nursing colleague and I served as associate chairs for the department (she in curriculum, and me in administration). She was just completing her doctorate in education degree, and this seemed like a "marriage made in heaven." It became more like the pits of hell. Beware of those feelings. Academia can be a viper pit. Especially if you are one of the only two males represented in the department.

We served in the roles, and all went on very well. The school had obtained a long-term lease on an adjacent property, formerly a long-term care facility. The plan was to move nursing into the building. Serving in the role of associate chair for administration I was involved in the planning and development of the simulation lab space and facilities. The school and program were moving ahead very nicely. Following the move, we were given new titles as associate deans. Once again, things were moving along nicely.

My colleague did take this opportunity to share, the "sisters" would never allow a "man" to be dean of the nursing program. Something wasn't right. I was immersed in my work and loved lifting the students. Something that was missing from the nursing department for many years.

Succession planning is so important, little did I know I would be bringing on the woman who would take my place.

Have faith in the Lord your God and you will be upheld; have faith in his prophets and you will be successful.

2 Chronicles 20:20 (NIV)

Time would pass, the department and program seemed to be moving in a very positive and wonderful direction.

At the end of the day, it was truly a blessing to retire and move forward. I was provided so many more wonderful opportunities and now work with positive individuals who are truly student and nursing advocates. I took with me so many wonderful memories, and because I was always there for the students that is what remains important for me. Let me share with you a few student remarks through the years.

Dr. Blair, from my first semester with you, you unequivocally believed in me. You are without a doubt an astonishing teacher, mentor, and friend. I truly thank you for that. I wouldn't be standing here right now without your encouragement and support.

J. D. – Student Speaker

White Tea Pinning Ceremony Class of 2018

Dr. Blair has been helpful to our class in general, he makes us feel like we can, actually do it. He is a great educator and is always available to help us understand.

Unknown Student

Class of 2019

He is always very positive and encouraging.

Unknown Student

Class of 2019

Dr. Blair was always available and truly cared for every student and pushed us to be better nurses!

Unknown Student

Class of 2019

I appreciate Dr. Russ's teaching style. He is knowledgeable, passionate, and makes me feel as though he truly cares about his students learning his course material. It is unfortunate that he did not teach more senior level courses.

Unknown Student

Class of 2020

I loved our instructor's style of teaching! Not only did we learn the content of a singular level but the exercises encouraged us to work together as a team. This can be missing in our field, so it was multi-level beneficial. Oh, and it was FUN

Unknown Student Class of 2020

I will always remember the students who I met loving you. I heard a lot over the years, but you were a favorite.

Colleague (D.C.)

Finally, an RN! And much of the thanks goes to this man; his advice, wisdom and just being an all-around amazing educator is the reason why his office was always filled with stressed out students needing his compassion, support, and empathy. I don't know of many other colleges where the Dean was not only an administrator and professor, but also a highly regarded confidante by the student body...

D. Q. RN

Class of 2020

Doc Blair, we could always tell you truly cared. I don't think any of us could have done it without you. Thank you so much! Because of you, I will be a better nurse.

K. K. RN

Class of 2020

I had initially intended on taking this **"something wasn't right"** chapter in an entirely different direction, but the student remarks that I have shared are just a few and they kept on coming following my announcement to retire. They have ultimately held my focus on taking the high road related to this adversity. As you will see later this adversity turned into a blessing. Probably much to the chagrin of those who initiated it. During a period of my morning devotions I felt, "something wasn't right" and then I suddenly recalled First Lady Michelle Obama stating, "when they go low, we go high." So that is the direction I went and continue to head. I would encourage you to also take the high road.

163

*"Love your neighbor and hate your enemy."
But I tell you, love your enemies and pray for
those who persecute you, that you may be
children of your Father in heaven.*

Matthew 5:43-45 (NIV)

*The Lord is close to the brokenhearted and
saves those who are crushed in spirit.*

Psalm 34:18 (NIV)

I retired May 15th and life has been amazingly wonderful. God has continued to provide and give me opportunities. And in my opinion, it is all to his glory. I have been given the opportunity and enjoy the experience of working with some of the best nationally and internationally known professional nurses and health care professionals, who truly exemplify nursing, serve as student advocates, and work to inspire others.

*When evildoers came against me to devour my
flesh, my foes and my enemies stumbled and
fell. Though an army deploys against me, my
heart will not be afraid; though a war breaks
out against me, I will still be confident.*

Psalms 27:2-3

Once again, God has our paths completely mapped out.

Take delight in the Lord, and he will give you the desires of your heart.

Psalm 37:4 (NIV)

That's why I work and struggle so hard, depending on Christ's mighty power that works within me.

Colossians 1:29 (NLT)

Do not be anxious about anything, but in every situation, by prayer and petition, with thanksgiving, present your requests to God, And the peace of God, which transcends all understanding, will guard your hearts and your minds in Christ Jesus.

Philippians 4:6-7 (NIV)

"Something wasn't right." Starting at age 50, men should have an annual "PSA." This is a marker to monitor for prostate cancer. Over the years, mine had hovered at borderline and in 2017-2018 it remained elevated. My urologist recommended a biopsy and referred me to a urology oncologist, who was simply amazing. He was involved in the "latest and greatest" of procedures. My first biopsy would be scheduled following an MRI if the MRI indicated a need. This new method would identify any questionable areas and the biopsy could be performed on those specific areas. The results of the MRI came back and there were several questionable areas. The first biopsy was completed, and the results were positive for "cancer." That ugly "C" word. Listening to the advice of my medical provider, his recommendation was to observe for a year as the current scoring for the cancerous areas was not the worst. Should there be any changes in the year, we would then discuss another plan.

Then your light will break forth like the dawn, and your healing will quickly appear; then your righteousness will go before you, and the glory of the Lord will be your rear guard.

Isaiah 58:8 (NIV)

In the same way, the Spirit helps us in our weakness. We do not know what we ought to pray for, but the Spirit himself intercedes for us through wordless groans.

Romans 8:26 (NIV)

The year passed and my annual PSA result remained elevated. My provider recommended a repeat MRI. Once again, the questionable areas remained evident, and another biopsy was scheduled. The biopsy was completed.

The cancer had progressed, and a radical robotic prostatectomy was recommended and scheduled. Life stood still. My father had bladder cancer and a transurethral resection of his prostate years prior, and I recalled the difficulties he experienced following surgery. It is in these times when being a healthcare professional may not be in our own best interest from a psychological perspective. My mom was simply beside herself and the "worry gene" was evident. I had viewed the surgical procedure several times via the internet. I understood the procedure. At this point I was looking at the bright side. My provider had told me, had I gone any place else for the biopsies they would have declared me "cancer free." According to my health care provider "the cancer is not in a typical place where we go for a biopsy." Had the MRI not been completed, and a "blind" biopsy been performed, the tumor would have been missed.

Give thanks to the Lord, for he is good; his love endures forever.

Psalm 107:1 (NIV)

So, here we are. Late summer, early fall 2018 and I have cancer. Not only do I have cancer, I need a major surgical procedure. I was

167

blessed to have one of the finest surgeons who performed the surgery. I understood the procedure, possible complications, and even the possible long-term effects following surgery. I have a major decision, not complying with the specialist and "taking my chances" or moving forward and placing my faith in my God's intervention. Following many discussions with a colleague who lost her husband to prostate cancer. I moved forward. I am grateful for those conversations.

Now faith is confidence in what we hope for and assurance about what we do not see.

Hebrews 11:1 (NIV)

In early December 2018 the surgery was completed. My wife and youngest son accompanied me to the hospital. They were told I would be done in three hours. Over five hours later, I was finally in recovery, and they would see me soon. I am certain over those hours many prayers were said. Once again, I believe my mom even at 93 was on her knees.

And pray in the Spirit on all occasions with all kinds of prayers and requests. With this in mind, be alert, and always keep on praying for all the Lord's people.

Ephesians 6:18 (NIV)

168

I followed the surgeon's instructions before surgery and had every intent on following what was going to be ahead, with-the-exception-of, "wearing depends." That was not happening. During this time, I was teaching, and would have been mortified if there was an accident while in front of the class. I took necessary precautions, but I never wore "Depends." A success! The surgeon was impressed. My post-surgical progress has been nothing but amazing and without complication. I stayed on course and did as I was instructed. I am truly thankful for those who prayed. I certainly know my mother was home with the bible open and her hands to God.

Be pleased to save me, Lord; come quickly; Lord, to help me.

Psalm 40:13

I know my mom was at the front of the prayer chain and talking with Jesus for weeks. Following discharge from the hospital I was visited by the pastor of a local church. Today he is my Pastor.

I am certain before the end of my days and before the end of your days, we will again experience, "something isn't right." I pray that my God will continue to bless us and provide us the guidance to move forward. I pray for the wisdom to know when "something isn't right" and to take the action desired by my God. Thankfully today I can say I am a cancer survivor, and I am grateful!

For the Lord gives wisdom; from his mouth comes knowledge and understanding. He holds success in store for the upright, he is a shield to those whose walk is blameless, for he guards the course of the just and protects the way of his faithful ones.

Proverbs 2: 6-8 (NIV)

So why did I share these life stories with you? Each one was an adversity that I had to overcome. Each one could have resulted in something worse or something better. In every case (and fortunately for me) the adversity resulted in moving forward. Of course, when they were happening forward was the last place I believed I was headed. Now I know that the adversities we face may only be for a period and then the light will shine. I am not foolish enough to believe that this happens to everyone in every adversity. I can tell you that you must always believe in yourself and hold onto your dreams through each adversity. It is a matter of never giving up and then looking back to see where you came from. There were times when letting go would have been so much simpler. I am thankful that I held on. You too should continue to believe in you and always move toward your dreams. There is even a chance something better will happen. So, to that end.

"Do not remember the past events, pay no attention to things of old."

Isaiah 43:18

I will be the same until your old age, and I will bear you up when you turn gray. I have made you, and I will carry you; I will bear and rescue you.

Isaiah 46:4

Sometimes you have a dream of achieving a goal and then God lets you in on a surprise. You get something much better than what you expected.

You may ask: How do we deal with wrongs against us? Pray thankfully to God and walk in love, forgiveness, and not vengeance. Show mercy even when others are unable to show mercy to you. When they go low, you go high. Go to the highest, your faith, your God! This is the thing. My God wants me to help someone else. Nothing can take away the reason for our existence or placement on earth.

No one can steal your memories and the wonderful things you experienced. Take the time to ponder those experiences. The light that is headed for you may be your bright future and not the train.

XII

Home

As my parents became older they hired help to mow the lawn, scrape away the snow and complete simple jobs around the house. I lived 40 minutes away, but when dad needed something urgently, I had to call one of my brothers-in-law to go and help him out.

He and mom lived in the family home until the autumn of 1999, when they purchased a modular home to install on my property. The mayor of our village was always supportive of what we were trying to do for my parents. Mom and dad moved in just before Halloween. She even decorated their new home for Halloween.

Prior to this they would stay with us in a room we had converted in the back of our garage. It was like a motel room with a fridge, toaster, microwave, and coffee maker. They would use a commode (something like a chamber pot in the days before flushing toilets became

173

common) and carry water. They had some special times with their grandsons in those days.

Dad had been suffering minor ailments for many years. His arthritis outdid everything else until it was painful watching a man — having built the family home from foundation to roof — become in need of help even with driving a nail to hang a picture for mom. Even though he continued to lose his strength, he was always excited about us spending a long weekend at the vacation condo in Lee, MA. No physical trouble was big enough to have him say no to travel.

He loved car rides and would generally sleep. If mom caught him dozing, she would ask what he was looking at and he always responded, "The deer."

I had no idea that dad's body would develop further problems. One afternoon, while he was packing, he staggered and fell face-first onto the concrete walkway bordering the pool. He fractured his nose and severely cut his face, hand and arms. The situation turned extremely painful for him when subsequently shingles sprouted on his skin. It was difficult for me as well because from there on, both his physical and mental health plunged.

Following that dreadful fall, dad continued to have one episode after another of falls and injuries. While making his bed, he fell between the bed and the wall, striking his elbow. I believe this was his final episode. He developed an infection in the skin, and he refused to go to the hospital. Thankfully, the family physician was able to provide the necessary supplies for us to care for my father at home. He needed a lot of stuff to dampen the pain.

A hospital bed was arranged to be brought into the house, and when we tried moving dad to it, he boomed: no, no, no. Even though he hadn't spoken in days, his voice did not crack at all on the stretcher as it was moved from his bedroom into the living room. There was no way he was going to the hospital, no sir. Mom and dad wanted to move from their earthly home into their heavenly home without any stopovers on the way.

On a cold January morning, the 5th, 2002, dad went on the journey to his heavenly home. His family was at the bedside. Mom had always worried about his heart, and it was the last thing to give out. I don't believe there ever was a reason to worry about dad's heart. He had the best!

We have all heard people speak about their loved one 'going home'.

A dark time that was. It was almost impossible to believe he was gone. When my parents passed away, first my dad and my mom much later, their spirits went on to cover the last lap of their journey home. What was left behind was an empty body for us to hand over to the bosom of the earth. For mom and dad, based on their Christian belief in God and Jesus Christ, they indeed passed from this home safely to their heavenly home. Nothing but that thought gets me through that dark time. Moreover, my belief that I too will join them when my work on earth is done braces my heart.

And he said to him, "Truly, I say to you, today you will be with me in Paradise."

Luke 23:43

The next several days were a blur. Dad indeed deserved the full military honors which he always wanted. He would have preferred to have been buried at the National Cemetery, but they had already purchased their eternal resting place. Passing in January in the northeast makes many final arrangements difficult. Dad was not buried until spring. An American flag was presented to my mom. I still

176

have it displayed today on our mantle with pride.

When I notified my nursing administrator of the passing of my dad, her first words were, "You know you only have three days." What did she say? I didn't need a response like that on top of the adversity that had befallen me. If that's the way you want to behave with an employee who is going through the death of a parent, I'd rather not imagine what kind of a personality they portrayed on a regular basis. But it's all a perspective. I was taken aback. I took all of fifteen days to feel ready enough to resume work. I survived. When you don't believe you can get through, know that you can. Following the passing of my father I interviewed for a promotion and I accepted the position at a facility nearly three hours from home.

I may not have done that had the interaction with the nurse administrator not pushed me to move forward. I most certainly would not have accepted it if dad still needed me. At the time mom was in an exceptional physical as well as mental state. But the opportunity may not come again for years. I knew that she wouldn't need me closer to home until much later. So, there you have it: adversity to success. I became a nurse administrator. This was the start of my administrative correctional health care career.

Although I was far from home, I had the support of family and friends who lived only 40 minutes from the facility where I was assigned for duty. They graciously opened their home for me as a place to stay during the 18 months I would be away from home. Success wouldn't have come to me without support.

The Lord is close to the brokenhearted and binds up their wounds.

Psalm 147:3

The love between mom and dad was truly special. Not a day went by that mom did not speak about him. We all missed him. His smile, his laugh, his advice, even his stubbornness was missed. I think mom missed the little arguments they would have in the evenings. Usually, they were over mom's sister. As time passed, all of us understood where dad had been coming from all those years. It was tolerated nonetheless, as it was mom's sister.

We had seen death before. This time it happened in our home. The death of a parent is a dismaying experience; for us it was a time we needed each other the most. Dad's passing left a huge hole in our hearts, especially for mom. Everyone was working at the time, so she was alone. She did have many visitors; everyone tried to fill in the gaps but obviously it wasn't the same thing. Learning to overcome our loss, we moved forward the best we could to make the darkness as frail as it was in our power to do so.

When I completed my doctoral program, she attended my commencement and doctoral hooding ceremony in New Orleans. She said that was her best vacation ever. I can still see her and my mother-in-law in their wheelchairs having a strawberry daiquiri at 10:30 in the morning.

Supporting mom and making dark times a bit brighter for her.

Mom had two things on her bucket list: Visit Alaska and go to Branson, Missouri. For her 90th birthday we were able to get her to Alaska.

A few weeks prior to the trip, mom had some pain in one of her knees. She had previously had both knees replaced. The orthopedic surgeon believed she may have a stress fracture near the prosthesis, so she was instructed to remain non-weight-bearing. She was transferred to a rehabilitation facility just

2-3 weeks prior to our scheduled cruise to Alaska.

The rehabilitation facility did not want to discharge her, and the physical therapist insisted the trip be rescheduled. The orthopedic surgeon had a different opinion by approving the trip if she did not place her full weight on her leg.

We were able to get mom discharged and she flew with us to Washington and then boarded the ship for her cruise to Alaska. Mom had asked if her sister could go. She came along and it would be mom's last trip with her sister. While on the cruise, mom's prosthesis and the shifting of her weight started a landslide of gastro-intestinal difficulties for her. Anxiety set in and I think that prevented her from having a fully enjoyable time. But my wife did an amazing job caring for her. From then onwards, mom always wanted her to provide the care. She never wanted me, even.

Despite her sister's antics it was a beautiful trip for mom and yielded many fond memories for me. I never did get mom to Branson. I know my sister and I carried her there in our hearts years later.

The darkest day of my life still lay ahead. It all began on Thursday, March 7th.

Dad wasn't the only one who suffered from tripping up and falling over. Mom had been doing well ever since a routine health care provider was assigned to visit at home. She had been moving around the house following a brief illness.

The legacy of lurching somewhere somehow to topple down to the floor had plagued my sister too. Her traumatic fall left her with a fractured ankle and she retired. Now she was tending to our mother's needs. It was heartening for me that my sister was staying with mom. I felt comfortable with my sister staying with mom and this allowed me to continue concentrating on my work.

Then, my mom moved from being a recovering patient to a care provider. Her sister, now 92 years old, fell and fractured her arm. This rendered her helpless. Imagine not being able to use your dominant arm at that age. The medical providers in the emergency department seriously recommended a rehabilitation center to her but like my dad, she wanted nothing of that. Unlike any other reasonable and responsible individual would have done, she came back to stay with my mom. If only she'd agreed to stay at the hospital, it would have spared mom the physical deterioration caused by caring for her. Somehow, I believe mom began her backward slip when she was placed in that badly timed position.

Mom had frequent accidents because her sister's feet were in the way of accessing the bathroom. My wife would ask mom's sister to move to another chair and assist her in transferring herself. But each time my wife went back, she found mom's sister in front of the bathroom door once again.

All this took place while I attended a memorial service in Florida for a lifetime friend of the family. Had I been home, I know I would have prevented this situation. Firmly advocating for my mother, I would—like any reasonable individual should—never put up with my mom providing care for an aging sibling. Why should she, after her own overwhelming condition following a hospital stay? Sadly, I wasn't home when the arrangements were made and during those eight weeks mom couldn't get adequate time to recover from her prior hospitalization.

When the 'me' become paramount, it blinds you. Everything unsuited to your comfort can go out the window. To her own detriment, Mom lived up to her sister's want.

Everything was laid out for our trip to Florida. Of course, each time we thought we were ready to take mom, her condition swung the other way. Presently, we were hopeful about her progress.

On Friday my sister called and informed me that mom couldn't stand. Although the day before her primary care provider had visited her, she was having serious trouble putting any weight on her right leg.

So, I asked mom, "Why didn't you tell your provider this yesterday?"

She responded, "Because it didn't hurt yesterday."

Mom was a tough woman. You could count on it, no matter what. But we could all see the agony on her face. She couldn't hold back the tears, so we immediately called her provider back.

As long as she stayed in her recliner, you saw nothing. The moment she needed to stand to use the commode, or the provider moved her to check something, the pain screamed in her eyes. The slightest pressure to her leg and she winced like a child. It was excruciating to watch. You could see the result of 'it's all about me'.

Vacation was out of the question as mom needed us home. The provider determined mom had a spontaneous bleed causing her to bleed into her leg. She had been on anticoagulant medication for years to treat atrial fibrillation. The provider informed mom they could cut off the blood thinners, and in effect delay the internal bleeding. Then they would give her a transfusion.

Mom asked what could happen if they stopped the blood thinners. When she was informed it could lead her to have a stroke, she simply said, "I'm not having a stroke, just give me something for pain."

As I sat there, everyone moving around, saying things I didn't hear, doing things I didn't see, the only thought that stood out clear in my head was: was it all about me? Had I missed the chance to be near my mother while her health floundered?

I didn't insist she go to the hospital for intervention. I just sat there and listened as the plans formed around and without me. The morphine for her pain was started and this would be the beginning of the end. We watched mom, settle into a deep sleep and then her breathing became so moist it was both heartbreaking and horrifying. I am not a proponent of the morphine regimen without hospice care involved. This too was another adversity.

It was a weekend and mom couldn't be admitted on a weekend. The hospice program didn't admit on weekends. What! People don't die on weekends. It seemed like mom lingered for days. She seemed at peace, but her respirations and the secretions were unbearable at times.

Everyone did the best they could to keep her comfortable. I sat and watched. Somehow, I think I managed to snatch myself from the situation completely, severing the connection to that awful reality. I know I couldn't have made it alone had my immediate family not been at the bedside with me throughout the entire trial. Other than mom's great grandchildren, everyone in the family was with her — in many instances our lifetime friends too.

It was as if a paralysis corralled me, numbing me to inaction and ineptitude. My nursing skills of nearly 40 years didn't serve a purpose during those days.

I am thankful and grateful for the other nurses in the family. My wife held up the best she could, managing her own family and mine. I'm positive anyone else in her place would have gone haywire.

Our youngest son and his wife were examples of what awesome nurses are. They, along with my wife and our older son's wife, kept mom clean and comfortable. They transferred mom from her chair to the hospital bed, providing the most exceptional personal care.

Even when mom's final breath escaped her, and it was time to ascertain she was no longer there; my youngest son's wife stepped up to perform what was necessary. It must have been trying for her, but she did not flinch. The intimate compassion she showed, testified to how superb she was at pulling it off. Through the harshest adversity, we always had family.

Everyone spoke to mom. All of mom's immediate family told her it was okay for her to go and be with dad.

I believe mom was able to hear every word spoken at her bedside during those days. We all told her she would be missed, but we would be okay. She lingered and lingered. Why was this woman of faith, so full of love, suffering for days?

We later discovered her sister hadn't told her it was okay. My wife Leanne tried to talk her round to it. She refused to say to her sister (my mom) that she would be okay after mom was gone.

"I won't do that!" It was all about her. But of course, it wasn't and never would be.

March 12th, 2019, was the darkest day of my life.

Mom passed in the early morning, with her entire family at her bedside. Her favorite music played as she went to be with her husband, our father, and her heavenly father. Adversity, I have learned to live with. Perhaps you have heard the words: They lived a long and wonderful life.

Well perhaps they did, but when it's someone you love, you want to keep them around forever. Mom continues to keep an eye on us today.

Why do I share these events with you? Was it all about me and did I just let my mother slip away? I continue to come to grips with that adversity even as I write. Success lies in learning who you may count on in your life during your adversities. Success lies in being sure of the ones who are important for us in moving forward.

187

My friends, you must prioritize your friends' list. The 800 friends you have on Facebook can't rescue your sinking heart. Look to the family you shared your life with, or the lifetime friends you can call family. Sometimes someone will drive from mid-Massachusetts to Schuylerville, NY to show their love and support. The friends you grew up with stand beside you through thick and thin. It is the lifetime friend who comes all the way from Kentucky to be sure you are okay, and to give you love and support. They are the ones you can count on. They want to be part of the trying times as well as the joyful moments of your life. I know the meaning of success because I know who will be there for me and my family in the future.

Mom used to say, "Are you going to be able to look out at a dark house after your father and I are gone?"

Nearly thirty years ago that didn't seem likely. Today I have the house lights on a timer, to shoo away the empty darkness manning the rooms.

The house has been used as an Airbnb since mom's passing. "Gramma Roses." Mom is still taking care of me. My faith that I will see mom and dad in my heavenly home keeps me moving.

My biggest regret: I let it all be about me, even if for a moment. Not for a second in time do I wish this adversity on you. An inner voice speaks the truth when it tells me that while I waded through sorrow, Jesus saw my pain and wept with me.

The Lord is near the brokenhearted; he saves those crushed in spirit.

Psalms 34:18

Making it all about 'you' at the wrong time can take you to a very dark place. We can never get the time back. But be aware: if you can overcome this adversity, and never forget where you came from, you will make it through the darkest time.

XIII

The Visit

Today was the ninety-third day since mom's passing. I went to the cemetery for the first time alone today. I didn't cry. That was a major accomplishment. Seems I had been crying for days. As I walked from the grave of one family member to another, the thought that I was going to be among those laid to rest refused to go away. Nonetheless, the visit was quiet and peaceful. The longer I looked at each of the headstones, the more solemn became the realization: I could stand there all day if I wanted but none of them were going to rise and hug me.

Over the past four years now, I have visited the cemetery many times. I take care of flowers for Memorial Day like I promised mom. Not a single May has gone by without me placing the flowers by her grave.

The stones are cleaned, and all items from around her resting earth are duly removed in the fall. Winter lights are neatly strung up then and an illuminated cross and cardinal remain on the graves. It was a promise I made to my parents and grandparents. I am going to keep up with my promise until I would no longer need to walk through the cemetery gates. I hope one of my sons will take over when I no longer can.

Sometimes weekly and sometimes monthly — the visit is a drive through; stopping first at mom's feet then dad; at times even stopping by to have a look at the place they will lay me down when the time comes.

It mostly lasts a little over an hour. A simple visit but nothing beats it at giving me the feeling of still being close to them – if only for a moment. This too is probably an adversity. Death seems to be against us (the ultimate bad luck?). No matter how much you get used to it, you can't deny you had rather had them walking by your side.

"Where, O death, is your victory? Where, O death, is your sting?"

1 Corinthians 15:55

191

The sting occurs for those left behind. A former colleague told me just weeks following mom's passing, that I was grieving for much too long. What the hell? I didn't realize there was a time limit and there absolutely isn't. Take the time you need. What a heartless thing to say. Can you imagine this was coming from a nurse?

Perhaps this individual didn't have a good relationship with a parent and was able to get over their death faster. I can't imagine this nurse at the bedside of a dying patient.

I can assure you there is no time limit for grief. If your grief interferes with normal day-to-day functioning for an extended time, appropriate intervention should be sought out. Sometimes we may need a little help moving forward. I did!

A counselor provided me professional help. I had to write a letter telling mom I was sorry for not advocating for her as I normally would have in the past. The counselor encouraged me to convey through that letter all the things I wish I had said between March 7th and 12th of 2019. I read it to her at the graveside. This time I cleansed a lot of tears. This time, the visit was a much needed cleansing experience.

Everyone should have a counselor. I may have been sad, but I certainly was able to function. I returned to work and functioned exceptionally, even though some sad times persisted.

What makes the death of a loved one traumatic is when they pass in the winter months (and these are Northeast winters), forcing you to wait until spring to complete their internment. That is when you have to face the trauma again. Remember mom passed in March. We were unable to have an internment until May.

My lifetime friend Sue and her husband Phil offered to host a lunch in May following mom's internment. Even friends from out of town attended to provide support. Those wonderful experiences were my light in the darkest times.

I am grateful that having support through that time kept me going. I am grateful to mom's grandsons who were able to walk with her to her final resting place; and to John, Phil, and Owen, who stepped up to be there for me. They were so gentle and caring as they walked with my sons and mom. Mom's pastor, Pastor Scott, too, for being so understanding and supportive — that continues even today. Love and care flow from this young pastor's heart.

He will wipe away every tear from their eyes. Death will be no more; grief, crying, and pain will be no more, because the previous things have passed away.

Revelation 21:4

Journey through death and grief has been an adversity for me. It made me stronger by pushing me toward independence. I began to draw strength from within myself, and for myself. Whereas the cemetery visits are perhaps a time of refreshing my inner peace.

"Those who sow in tears will reap with shouts of joy."

Psalm 126:5

I have the letter and I have informed my wife that it should be placed with me when my time comes. Yes, it is okay for men to cry. Perhaps the world would be a better place if we all did.

I know this seems a bit out of sorts, but this exercise helped me find peace in the most difficult time of my life. I am thankful I initiated counseling to get me through this troubled period. Do I still have regrets? I believe I do. I continue to overcome this

194

adversity. But I have never forgotten where I came from.

XIV

Moving Forward

"Your purpose gives you strength to move forward even when times are tough. Purpose stabilizes your life. With a clear purpose, you persevere because you know there's a reason, a cause."

David Jeremiah

What is the one thing in your life that generates strength each time you run out of it? Have you discovered your purpose? What is your calling?

My calling has been to teach, to inspire, to lift up, and provide motivational stories that help move individuals (especially nursing students) forward.

I've had my sizeable share of losing sight of my purpose. Those times I honestly wanted to sink out of sight. You know how it feels, don't you? The strange thing about believing that such and such is one's purpose, is, you lose sight of it as soon as you attempt to validate it. Have any of you felt the same? This is an exercise in remembering it isn't all about "me."

"Don't be afraid, because I am with you. Don't be intimidated; I am your God.

I will strengthen you.

I will help you.

I will support you with my victorious right hand."

Isaiah 41:10

Following the passing of my mother in 2019, I strongly believed that my purpose was complete. Caring for mom and dad is what we did and did it well since 1999.

Sooner or later, motivation becomes something too squishy to hold on to. The harder you want to hold, the quicker it evades your grip. Shutting out every emotion then, to count what you've got on the list for moving on gives you more reasons put beside the ones telling you to sit still.

To maintain my stability, I keep my purpose at the forefront of my thinking. There are days I start believing what I am doing is somewhat of a burden to others. Then I realize I'm doing it for the good of others. I'm doing it because I hope to prepare them to be successful through their adversities.

I get reminded now and then that I'm terrible at retirement. I have retired twice and will hopefully continue to contribute until I am ready to fully retire at some point in the future.

As this world becomes increasingly negative, and fills up with hurt and pain, I believe it is important to lift people up. There is a lack of encouragement derived from positive experiences.

Dr. David Jeremiah stated: Purpose stabilizes your life — and so a clear purpose gives us a reason. How will you overcome your adversity if you're still ignorant of your purpose? Success means moving forward. Without purpose, why make any attempt to move forward?

I have had to impel myself forward on many occasions. I am certain each of you have. Was the first step forward easy? Did you meet anxiety and fear standing across your path? Did they let you pass without protest?

Therefore, I say to you, do not worry about your life, what you will eat or what you will drink; nor about your body, what you will put on. Is not life more than food and the body more than clothing?

Matthew 6:25

For God has not given us a spirit of fear, but one of power, love, and sound judgment.

2 Timothy 1:7

Anxiety in a person's heart weighs it down, but a good word makes it glad.

Proverbs 12:25

Anxiousness can destroy a person from the inside out. Lifting them up with a good word can make them glad. Isn't that what we should be doing for each other?

There arose plenty of opportunities in Slip ups and Trip ups for me to redefine my purpose. As I get older, I redefine my purpose nearly every day. I suspect I need to examine my purpose over and over to keep the motivation going.

I don't pretend to be an expert at psychology but I've seen that getting older demands a reexamination of a purpose that you took for granted earlier. Should I determine I have no purpose left? Not true! I have four beautiful grandchildren who give me purpose, daily. I have a family that gives me purpose.

Go find your purpose. It's out there. Grab it and sprint forward.

Haven't I commanded you: be strong and courageous? Do not be afraid or discouraged, for the Lord your God is with you wherever you go."

Joshua 1:9

Allow yourself to become for another that which they have trouble becoming for themselves. Help them make a connection to the senior group they need. Help them find the church group that might work something miraculous for them.

Show the ones you love that they make a difference. Keep them actively involved with family and community. I think one of the hardest things for mom was being alone after dad passed. Although we were close and visited daily, it was pre-retirement and my job required me to be on the road a lot of the time. Her home was lonely without dad. She even missed their little arguments. She overcame the adversity and lived to be ninety-four. She found her purpose and fulfilled it well.

"Even the darkness is not too dark for you. Night is as bright as day. Darkness and light are the same to you."

Psalm 139:12

XV

Today I Saw a Cardinal

I accompanied my sister today to the cemetery again to say hello to mom and dad at their graves. It still sounds surreal, and I still can't believe it is true. Can't really do much, I have been in such a fog. This is all just a bad dream. Our washer is still not repaired. That meant laundry at mom's house again. Haven't spent a morning reading my devotions or bible on mom's porch lately, but today I saw a cardinal.

All birds relate to spiritualism in some way or another. I have been told the cardinal is no exception. It is said the red cardinal can be a messenger. Their simplest message is to acknowledge that a loved one is always around. Mom was a lover of birds and bird watching. She would sit for hours and watch the birds at the feeders. Her most precious bird was the red cardinal. I suspect because her favorite color was red.

The red cardinal certainly held a special place in mom's heart. Spotting one was always very positive and uplifting for her. She could hear a cardinal singing when she couldn't hear dad talking when he may have been sitting right next to her. She always believed seeing a red cardinal was a direct sign from heaven that she was not alone; after dad's passing it was a sign that he was okay.

Prior to that, it was a sign from her mother. The red cardinal was a sign that her ancestors were watching over her. Mom's mother passed on Mother's Day which made that day an annual adversity for her. After facing a similar loss and seeing the red cardinal, it became a sign that mom was somehow still with me and still provided her support and compassion for me.

Now this could be all nonsense. I chose to believe it was true and was exactly what I needed at the time. Following her passing when I simply couldn't remove myself from the house, I would see cardinals every day.

Haven't seen many lately, but today I saw a cardinal. Someone visited from heaven. Filling my darkness with the brightest light.

203

XVI

The Conclusion/The Beginning

This book was initially intended to be a supportive guide for nursing students. I hope it developed into something more.

It's true I originally conceived this project because I was interested in helping nursing students become successful. I understand what their professional dreams are about. While writing, I realized I had more to share with my readers than I had originally thought. Looking back on my experiences and mulling over their outcomes, I decided something about my story might as well help those who didn't want to become nurses.

I never dreamed of being a nurse. Nursing was not even a thought among all the muddled dreams in my head. I used to think I wanted to be an elementary teacher. Time led me into nursing and it turned out to be the calling I never expected. As I entered the twilight of my

204

profession as a nurse, it did fulfill my desire of teaching. So I had my shot at teaching elementary nurses, if not elementary school kids.

I have been blessed by so many of my former students reaching the place they always dreamt they wanted to reach. Seeing them succeed has been wonderful. I am no stranger to the adversities of the academic setting, so it makes me especially happy to see those who made it through that phase.

Assisting others to keep moving through the dark phases of life has been a blessing and the highlight of my calling in life. Having been an underdog myself, I know what it involves. I so appreciate the trust each student had in me. I consider myself fortunate that I can still continue the role of advocacy. I believe in building up and not kicking someone when they are already down.

Writing this book has been a cleansing and learning opportunity for me.

It was cleansing, because it gave me a chance to talk about the dark places I got trapped in. I experienced intervention from the God who I have faith in and with whom I continue to develop my relationship. The relationship grows every day, because I work on it every day.

It was a chance to learn because as I placed scriptures on paper, I realized divine intervention is not a fantasy. It was startling to find my experiences reflected in the wisdom of the Bible. God makes it possible for you to follow the thread if you want to make the connection. This project made it easy to see how we can be guided by simply focusing on these special words.

The astounding aspect about each situation I shared is that there is something to derive from a biblical reference that will back the actions we should take or could have taken in that situation.

Someone has walked the same road as us; maybe even thousands of years ago. None of this is new. We can learn from the adversities of years past.

"Now, every time I witness a strong person, I want to know: What dark did you conquer in your story? Mountains do not rise without earthquakes."

Katherine MacKenett

"To dream anything that you want to dream…That is the beauty of the human mind. To do anything that you want to do…That is the strength of the human will. To trust yourself is to test your limits…That is the courage to succeed."

Bernard Edmonds (American Writer)

For I know the plans I have for you" – plans for your well-being, not for disaster, to give you a future and a hope.

Jeremiah 29:11

It has been my purpose through this journey to give you the tools necessary for you to develop a plan for your well-being, not your disaster, and in some way give you strength and hope for the future. You have seen the dark times in my story and I hope they can provide strength for you to move forward to the light.

Although this is 'The Conclusion,' perhaps it really is 'The Beginning.'

The beginning of you finding your purpose, moving forward, and seeing that your adversities can lead to your success.

"Everything has its own time, and there is a specific time for every activity under heaven."

Ecclesiastes 3:1

Is today your time?

The final question many of my students would ask: Dr. Blair, what words of wisdom do you have for us? Wow, what a question to ask. What an honor to have an opportunity to attempt a response.

Wisdom can be defined as the quality of having experience, knowledge, good judgment and being wise.

Wisdom, insight, perception, perceptiveness, understanding, and discernment; all these qualities connect with each other.

In the process of writing for you I may have discovered more of myself. I have discovered that there is not a time limit on grief. At times, we lack good judgment and an ability to demonstrate how wise we really are. We make mistakes. We will be unsuccessful. And we learn from those experiences. What is important and essential to remember is **you are not a failure**.

We may fall completely apart. The wisdom comes from having the insight, understanding, and perception to get back up and move forward. Sometimes this can take only a few minutes, while at other times it can be years.

Remember, I started this journey a long time ago. You may have started your journey this semester, this month, this week, or even today. I have learned that our purpose can change from day to day or minute to minute and that is how we continue to move forward.

I have made mistakes and I am certain you have as well. It remains evident that we can move forward and work at becoming better. We can be better for our community, better for our families and most importantly, we can be better for ourselves. We need to love ourselves before we can love anyone or anything else.

You and I have known times when our legs were cut completely out from under us. We have all been there. Yet we are here to talk about it and we are working to move forward.

Through my dark times, I remember:

- The adversity when they gave me up for adoption as soon as I yelled for breath in the air outside my birth mother's womb. That resulted in the success of finding loving parents and a wonderful life.

- The adversity that I wasn't "college material" and the motivation that statement provided for me later in life. All I had to do was to wait.

- The adversity of my dad having a heart attack and my vision of working for him in a paper mill vanishing. The event led to entering a practical nursing program and ultimately an amazing career.

- The adversity of being unsuccessful in my first attempt on the clinical performance exam. It resulted in working on previous mistakes and succeeding on the second attempt. It also resulted in gaining many wonderful students. I was not a failure, and neither are they.

- The adversity when they conned me into paying for a degree issued by a college that never existed. I motivated myself to start from the beginning once again. Later, I walked across the stage at my Doctoral Commencement Ceremony to receive a degree from a regionally accredited university. With it came the rights, honors, privileges, and responsibilities of that degree.

- The adversity of being a marginal student throughout my elementary and high school years motivated me to achieve an advanced terminal degree later in life.

- The adversity when loved ones passed away but I gained a better perspective on my purpose and the ability to move forward. Without forgetting where I came from.

- The adversity of COVID-19 and the changes I went through to become an instructor for nursing students. It resulted in finding out my true calling. I developed and nationally presented education courses for the ultimate nursing organization.

Wisdom? We all have wisdom to share. What is your wisdom? Just remember:

"Never forget where you came from."

Dr. Russell Blair

Through my adversities I managed to move forward to where I am today. Although not as positive then about my purpose as I am today, I have kept moving forward. This is what your goal should be as well. I have been in some dark places and now I must share some of the beautiful things I have accomplished during the journey.

Life is not fair all the time. Sometimes we are dealt a bad hand, but the key is to keep playing. Never give up and never quit. I was adopted by the most wonderful people anyone could ask for: A mom and dad who both loved to live and wanted that for everyone. I can remember my mom telling dad in a grocery line to pay for the groceries of the man in front of them because he didn't have enough money. My mother caught insects in tissue paper and put them outside rather than killing them.

I believe I was stubborn but I kept falling back on my faith. When I made the decision to fully retire from an academic setting, I knew deep down I wasn't ready to settle into that rocking chair on the front porch. I kept my foot in academia by serving as an adjunct clinical nursing instructor for a local practical nursing program. I later served as a classroom instructor for the same program during a fall/winter semester. I also was able to serve as an adjunct professor of nursing in a graduate nursing program. I never forgot where I came from.

"He gives strength to those who grow tired and increases the strength of those who are weak."

Isaiah 40:29

Nearly three years ago, I responded to a LinkedIn ad for a Content Author. I could write content, so I submitted my curriculum vita (CV). I received a call from an organization. I recognized the name from a previous purchase. I had purchased tickets for a cruise conference prior to COVID-19 and it had been postponed a couple of times. What I didn't realize was the connection between the two. I do today, and the adversity of leaving academia has resulted in being part of an ultimate nursing organization, as a nurse planner, author, and educator. I have the honor of working with a team of professionals that care about what they are doing and they prepare the nurses of the future. It's an amazing organization that truly supports and encourages nurses in a safe environment.

My support and drive to lift people couldn't have found a better match. I have presented during the conferences and this opportunity has afforded me the opportunity to fulfill my

213

calling and purpose. I continue to move forward, and I have never forgotten where I came from. I believe that has made a difference. I got to where I am today because of that motto. Not bad for an orphan who was left behind?

"Once you lived in the dark, but now the Lord has filled you with light. Live as children who have light."

Ephesians 5:8

I encourage you to build a barrier between yourself and potential disasters that make you lose sight of your purpose in life. Allow yourself to grow. Things can be better if you allow yourself time to heal. I can't be certain where tomorrow will take me or even if I will be around to see tomorrow. What I am certain of is that the adversities of life can lead to successes. You must always have faith in yourself and never give up on your dreams.

Everything is possible for the one who believes."

Mark 9:23

I told mom from time to time, "I don't know what I want to do when I grow up." What I do know is I will never forget where I came from, and neither should you.

I know I will have more adversities in my life, but I hope to be better prepared in handling them. Some adversities may last a lifetime, but we must not allow them to prevent us from life.

Any clinical scenario I ever share with nursing students, I ask them to do some form of reflection on the scenario. I am going to request that you do the same. Through the pages of this book, I tried to provide you with something to reflect on. Take time now to reflect on the amazing and wonderful things that you experienced during your journey.

You may think you're faced with an adversity that is impossible to overcome, but you've already had many wonderful surprises, joys, and outcomes. What lies ahead for you is even better! I wish you all the successes life has in store for you.

"Sometimes the most difficult road will lead to a beautiful destination. The best is yet to come."

Zig Ziglar

"You can get there from here, don't give up on faith."

Mark209

Dear reader, I hope reading this far has made you believe that you can find a solution to the puzzle of your future.